FROM PASCAL TO C

An Introduction to the C Programming Language

Douglas L. Brown
University of Houston, Clear Lake

'shing Company
'ifornia
'sworth, Inc.

Signing Representative: Terry Baxter
Computer Science Editor: Frank Ruggirello
Designer: Sara Hunsaker
Editorial Production Service: Ex Libris

Cover Designer: John Edeen
Cover Photograph: Computer graphics image "Softy 1" © Frank Dietrich

Printed in the United States of America

2 3 4 5 6 7 8 9 10 —— 89 88 87 86 85

Library of Congress Cataloging in Publication Data

Brown, Douglas L.
From Pascal to C.

Includes index.
1. C (Computer program language) I. Title.
QA76.73.C15B76 1985 001.64′24 84-25662

ISBN 0-534-04602-9

PREFACE

The Purpose of This Text

The C programming language is a powerful and concise language and is often the language of choice for systems programmers. The popular operating system UNIX is written in C, and the language will be used increasingly in coming years.

For years, though, the only textbook on C available was *The C Programming Language*, by Brian Kernighan and Dennis Ritchie. Although elegant and advanced, Kernighan and Ritchie is primarily a reference work and not the introductory text that many of us need.

This book is intended to provide that introduction to C, leading you in a logical progression from the simplest elements of the language to its more complex features. The book begins with a brief review of the language's history and then proceeds to a discussion of C program structure, data types, and fundamental control structures. It continues with a discussion of more advanced topics, including the use of pointers and structures. A complete description of C syntax and grammar is provided, and each chapter contains numerous examples of C code.

ique Feature—Relating C to

ne particular feature of this text makes it unique. I assume that C is not
ır first programming language. (It is unlikely that C is anyone's first pro-
nming language!) I particularly assume that you are familiar with the
amming language Pascal.

each element of C is presented, it is compared with the corresponding
in Pascal. Many of the examples in the text are presented in both C
al. If you understand Pascal, you should be able to program in C
quickly. I have tried to make the transition from Pascal to C as
possible; if you are familiar with a particular construct in Pascal,
able to find and build the equivalent construct in C easily.

Programming Examples

Each chapter of this text outlines some specific element of C—program structure, data types, control structures. As elements are described, simple examples illustrating the use of each element are provided. Some examples are program fragments, and others are short programs.

At the end of each chapter, a more significant programming example is provided. These are designed to illustrate both the use of C in a programming environment and the concept of "software tools." Software tools are short programs that perform useful functions and that can be combined with other "tools" to perform larger functions. The generation of these tools is a common use for C.

To reinforce the concepts presented, each chapter also includes a number of programming exercises. These exercises may further develop the short programs used as examples in the chapter, or they may use the programming concepts introduced to develop new applications.

C in the UNIX Environment

Many C programmers reading this book will be using the language in a UNIX environment. To help those programmers, I have included a description of important UNIX utilities, including UNIX editors and the UNIX C compiler. I have also described the system input and output capabilities available under UNIX and provided examples of file manipulations under UNIX.

Appendixes and Supplementary Materials

In addition to leading you sequentially through the elements of the C programming language, this text provides reference materials that summarize some of this information. A summary of C syntax as well as the following appendixes are included.

—list of C reserved words
—use of the C preprocessor
—C compilers for microcomputers
—list of C references
—examples of a systems-level C program

A Final Word

Learning C is not a difficult task. This book will provide you with a soun
understanding of the basic elements of the language. Read the book, work t
exercises, and in time you will find that you understand the language we
And remember . . . on a clear day, you can C forever!

Acknowledgments

This text has been shaped by many individuals, and it is impossible to thank them all. I thank my professors at the University of Wisconsin; without them, I would never have seen the need for this book. I thank David Chappell and Alan Burke, my colleagues at Wisconsin; without their support and comments, the text would not have been as organized and error-free as it is. I thank my reviewers, whose knowledge and care have refined the text greatly: Terry A. Ward, University of Northern Iowa; Charles "Pat" Reynolds, James Madison University; Samuel Coppage, Old Dominion University; Alan Feuer; Michael Levy, University of Victoria; Stuart T. Teges, Stanford University; Wesley F. Mackey, Florida International University; Hussein Abdel-Wahab, Old Dominion University. I thank Kernighan and Ritchie, whose elegant book serves as the standard against which all others are measured. I thank Frank Ruggirello, senior editor at Wadsworth Publishing Company, whose encouragement and dedication to this project have been crucial. And I thank my wife, Judi, for her endless patience and understanding during all those nights at the computer!

Douglas L. Brown
Houston, Texas

CONTENTS

CHAPTER 1

A Quick Look at C, UNIX, and Pascal

C AND UNIX

Where did the programming language C come from, and why are people so interested in it? C was developed in 1972 by Dennis Ritchie at Bell Laboratories. The roots of C can be found in a language called BCPL (developed in the 1960s at MIT and Cambridge) and its successor, B. BCPL was a typeless language; it only permitted one data object (the machine word), and some of C's central features can be traced to BCPL. Like Pascal, C is classified as a high-level language and is a relative of Algol. In Figure 1.1 you can see the relationship between Algol and some of the other languages that are similar to it.

Most programs that can be written in Pascal could also be written in C. However, whereas Pascal was designed in part as a vehicle for teaching computer science and structured programming, C was intended for more pragmatic uses and includes features that are not part of Pascal. We will discuss these features in more detail later, but they include the ability to perform bit-level manipulations and other low-level operations required for systems programming.

Systems programming, the design and coding of large programs such as operating systems and compilers, was a major target area for C. These kinds of programs had historically been written in assembly language. The programs needed to run as efficiently as possible, and coding them at a low level produced the fastest and most flexible programs. C, however, is a high-level language that produces fast, compact object code, and the use of C permits development of systems-level programs without resorting to assembly language programming.

There had been earlier efforts, notably PL/I, to design a high-level lan-

FIGURE 1.1 Schematic genealogy for members of the Algol family of languages.

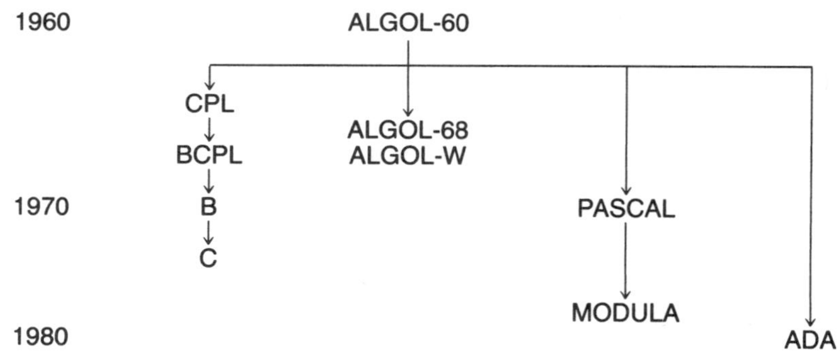

guage that could be used for systems programming, but the results were judged, perhaps unfairly, as unsuccessful. (MULTICS, an innovative operating system designed at MIT in the mid-1960s, was written in PL/I, but it proved to run too slowly for many intended applications.) It became clear, however, as the power and complexity of systems programs increased, that the machine inefficiencies associated with writing in a high-level language were at least partially offset by great gains in human efficiency and by an increase in program reliability. With increasing machine speeds, the programmer's time became at least as valuable as the machine's time, and the advantages of high-level systems programming began to outweigh the disadvantages.

C has proven to be a language that offers the advantages of high-level programming as well as program efficiency approaching that of assembly language. This success is partly due to the fact that C is a terse language; it provides only the bare essentials, but from those a rich variety of applications can be derived. In addition, some of the language's operations are close to machine-level; for instance, some of the C operations have direct equivalents in PDP-11 assembly language. The result is that a C compiler can produce fast, compact code in the PDP-11 environment that approaches the speed of an assembly-language program.

The development of the UNIX operating system was an early demonstration of the strength of this approach. (The name, by the way, is a play on the name MULTICS.) The first incarnation of UNIX was written by Ken Thompson in 1970, and the succeeding version, written by Thompson and Dennis Ritchie in 1972, was produced almost entirely in C. The success and widespread popularity of UNIX are convincing evidence that the design goals of the language have been achieved. Today UNIX and C are closely linked, and it is difficult to discuss one without the other.

UNIX is a relatively small, interactive operating system intended to facilitate the development and testing of both system and application programs. However, UNIX is more than just an operating system. It is a complete programming environment that is built around a consistent philosophy and that contains many available "software tools." These tools include a concise and powerful editor, many easily accessed system utilities, an electronic mail system, and (most relevant to our purposes) a C compiler.

UNIX has expanded from Bell Labs to widespread use on minicomputers in universities and the rest of the computing community. By late 1983, over 5500 installations had been licensed to use UNIX source code, and there were many more sublicenses for the binary code. It has even been flattered by imitation, with several look-alikes (such as XENIX and IDRIS) currently available for use on microcomputers. UNIX was first implemented on a DEC PDP-7 computer, but versions now exist for many different machines, including microcomputers. Currently, the most common home for UNIX is probably the DEC PDP-11 series of minicomputers.

As the number of UNIX environments increases, so does the popularity of C. The upsurge of interest in C, though, is not solely the result of its connections with UNIX. Programmers who need access to the machine at a lower level than permitted by languages such as Pascal are increasingly choosing to write in C. The number of C compilers that run in non-UNIX environments continues to grow. Fortunately, despite the growing number of compilers, C has largely managed to avoid the standardization problems common to other widely used languages. Most versions are very similar; where differences exist, we will attempt to point them out.

SIMILARITIES BETWEEN C AND PASCAL

C and Pascal are distinctly different languages, and each has specific strengths and weaknesses. When programs in the two languages are compared, however, they may appear at first to be very similar. In fact, it's possible to write a program in both C and Pascal and have the results appear (after allowing for relatively minor syntax differences) essentially identical. Figure 1.2 illustrates this similarity with a program written in both languages. (Ignore temporarily the details of the C program and note the broad similarities.) The two languages do share a common philosophy of program structure and some common control structures, thus producing a similar appearance. It also makes C relatively easy to learn if you are already familiar with Pascal.

For instance, both languages are **subprogram oriented**. A Pascal program consists of a set of procedures and functions and a block of code that serves as the main program. A typical C program will consist of a set of functions; C has no provision for distinct "procedures" and "functions" but instead uses functions for both types of subprogram. In a C program, one of these

FIGURE 1.2 The same program written in C and Pascal; each version looks similar to the other.

Pascal program:

```
program firstdemo (input, output);
var a : integer;

(* main program code *)
begin
     a := 10;
     while (a < 10) do
          a := a * a;
end.
```

C program:

```
#include <stdio.h>
int a;

/* main function code */
main()
{
     a = 10;
     while (a < 10)
          a = a * a;
}
```

component functions has the function name **main**, and this block of code corresponds to the main-program code found in a Pascal program. Figure 1.3 illustrates a very simplified view of C and Pascal program structure.

Pascal and C also handle variables in similar ways. Both languages require that variables and variable types be declared, and similar syntax is used in both languages for type declarations. Both languages also provide for pointer data types. C and Pascal have similar scoping rules for variables, and the provisions for global and local variables in both languages are similar.

In addition, the two languages have several control structures in common. It is possible to express most commonly encountered structures (including "if. .then. .else," for loops, while loops, repeat loops, and case statements) in both languages, and the actual syntax used for the structures is often very similar.

Like Pascal, C is also a **free-format** language. Program files are created with any convenient editor, and the actual placement of code on a line in the program is left to the programmer, with statements generally ending with a ";". (There is a subtle difference in the way that C and Pascal use semicolons,

FIGURE 1.3 Simplified C and Pascal program structure.

Pascal skeleton	C skeleton
⟨program heading⟩	⟨program heading⟩
⟨procedure . . . ⟩	⟨main function⟩
⟨procedure . . . ⟩	
⟨procedure . . . ⟩	⟨function . . . ⟩
⟨function . . . ⟩	⟨function . . . ⟩
	⟨function . . . ⟩
⟨main program code⟩	⟨function . . . ⟩

which is taken up in Chapter 2.) There are no restrictions, as in FORTRAN and COBOL, about the physical placement of program code on a line.

Despite these superficial similarities, the two languages do differ on a number of significant points, a fact that becomes obvious when a C program is analyzed in detail. In some areas, C reflects the very different needs of systems programming, needs that result in distinct language features.

DIFFERENCES BETWEEN C AND PASCAL

One programmer's feature is another's bug. Both C and Pascal have several distinctive features—but what C may claim as a feature might easily be mistaken by a Pascal programmer as a bug. Veteran C programmers respect and appreciate those special features that give this language its distinct flavor and realize that they reflect the basic needs of the systems programmer. In general, those features give the programmer total control and permit the construction of optimally efficient object code.

For instance, C permits (and even encourages) the construction of very terse source code. If a Pascal programmer casually peruses a listing of a C program, the conciseness allowed by the language is immediately apparent. Although not as terse as APL, C programs can compact a great deal of meaning into a single function or even into a single line (Figure 1.4). This brevity can be a real boon to an experienced programmer who is well-versed in the subtleties and shades of meaning that the language allows. There's a certain attraction in writing that would be a 200-line COBOL program in 30 lines of C.

On the other hand, this near-telepathic style can lead the careless programmer to unwanted side-effects and some very insidious errors. Many C

FIGURE 1.4 A little C code can do a lot.

Very concise C code:

```
while (( ans = swap (first,second))>0)
```

Meaning of code:
- Call function 'swap' with arguments given
- Function is executed
- Result is returned and assigned to 'ans'
- If ans > 0, then repeat while loop again

operators are legal in several different contexts, sometimes with meanings that may seem unnatural to Pascal programmers. Different (and sometimes unrelated) tasks can be performed in a single line. Even seasoned programmers may find themselves investing a significant amount of time trying to understand someone else's code . . . or code that they themselves have written in the past! Pascal programs are, on the whole, much more readable because they don't encourage this terse style.

Another difference between C and Pascal is the relative emphasis placed on **reliability** and **flexibility**. Although both are worthwhile goals, they are emphasized very differently in the two languages. C permits great programming flexibility and sacrifices (to some extent) program reliability; the C programmer has great control over the machine's operations. Pascal produces programs that are reliable, but not as flexible.

Throughout the UNIX system the implicit assumption is made that you, the programmer, know what you're doing. The UNIX system and its tools are there to help you, even if what you're doing is somewhat unorthodox. C, which can be considered perhaps the most powerful of the UNIX tools, follows this assumption. The language is designed to be powerful and flexible; it is also designed to be small. As a result, many features that would strengthen the reliability of a program are not included.

For instance, a Pascal programmer would probably expect a language to check whether a function is called with the correct number of arguments. Failure to check this would be regarded as a bug. In C, however, neither a compile-time nor a run-time error message is generated by a program that defines a function as having two arguments and then later calls the function with three.

Likewise, a Pascal programmer would probably expect a language to check array bounds. In C, however, an attempt to read from the twenty-first element of an array that had been declared to be of size twenty will not produce an error message. This is because array subscripts in C are not automatically checked against the array's declared bounds, as they are in Pascal.

In general, C doesn't approach the level of "hand-holding" that Pascal provides. C programmers must do more of their own error-checking than if they were programming in Pascal, but they gain greater flexibility. What is lost is the greater built-in reliability of a Pascal program.

Nowhere is this tradeoff more evident than in the area of type-checking. Pascal enforces strict rules about types, whereas C again assumes that the programmer knows what he or she is doing.

The type of a variable determines the interpretation of the bit-pattern in the memory locations associated with that variable's name. For example, referring to a variable declared to be of type "integer" will result in the bits stored at that variable's memory location being interpreted using the code for integers (usually the binary number system). Referring to a variable of type "character" will cause the bits in the referenced location to be interpreted using the code for characters (usually ASCII or EBCDIC). Many languages, including both C and Pascal, also allow the programmer to create new types; these user-defined types are made up of combinations of the predefined types supplied by the language or of groups of arbitrary objects.

If a language tightly restricts the circumstances in which a location associated with a variable of one type may be interpreted as a different type, the language is said to be **strongly typed**. Pascal is strongly typed; C, with its different purposes, is not. Interpreting a value of one type as a different type (sometimes called **representation viewing**) is accomplished in Pascal mainly through the use of variant records. C, on the other hand, allows representation viewing in many contexts; a given location can be interpreted as being several different types (Figure 1.5). This flexible interpretation of data is essential for systems programming, but it can cause subtle bugs. Strong typing decreases flexibility but improves reliability.

The decrease in reliability caused by C's loose approach to types and other "features" can be offset by the use of one of UNIX's tools. This tool is a program called **lint**, which can be thought of as a C compiler that produces only error messages. The lint program will scan a C source file for possible errors and

FIGURE 1.5 C permits multiple interpretations of a memory location.

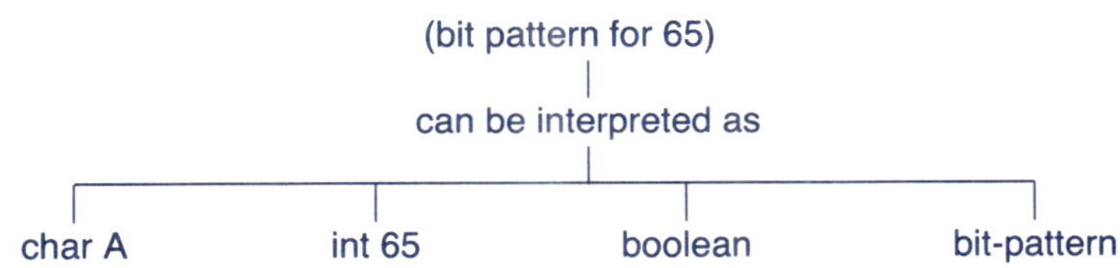

print out a report on possible errors. It does much of the checking that a strict compiler would do; it warns of type mismatches, uninitialized variables, and other possible errors. In fact, the only real difficulty in using "lint" is in sifting through the mass of output to find warnings that are really meaningful! Nevertheless, if you are working on a UNIX system, we strongly recommend the use of lint. It detects many of the errors that a Pascal programmer, who is used to a more rigorous compiler, might otherwise have trouble detecting.

EXERCISES

1. When, where, and by whom was the C language developed? What was its primary intended purpose?
2. The UNIX operating system is a programming environment in which C is often found. Identify other environments in which C is currently implemented. (Use other reference sources that may be available to you.)
3. Both C and Pascal are procedure-oriented languages and make available local as well as global variables. Make a table comparing the availability of procedures and scoping in FORTRAN 77, COBOL-65, BASIC (and other languages available to you).
4. What is meant by "strongly typed"? In Pascal, how can a memory location be referenced by variables of different types? Give one example.
5. Pascal provides two kinds of subprograms. Why does C provide only one kind? What differences do you think this will create in C programs?
6. C does not provide much of the error-checking provided by Pascal. Why?
7. What is the program "lint"? Why should it be used when programming in C?

CHAPTER 2

The Structure of a C Program

SOME INITIAL THOUGHTS

Although C programs and Pascal programs have similar structures, some differences are immediately obvious. Both languages lend themselves to structured programming techniques, and both are subprogram oriented. However, whereas Pascal programs contain procedures and functions as basic component subunits, C programs use only functions as basic subunits. This chapter will examine the basic structure of a C program and compare it with the structure of a similar Pascal program.

Figure 2.1 provides a starting point for the comparison, outlining a typical C program and a typical Pascal program. Pascal has a more rigid program structure, with careful specification of the order in which various elements must occur. C, characteristically, is more flexible, allowing some variation in the ordering and placement of sections of the code. For example, the main program in Pascal must be at the end of the program, since procedures or functions referenced by the main code must have been defined previously. In C, the **main** function may be placed anywhere in the program, although a common style is to place it at the beginning of the program.

Other differences exist in the structure of the two languages and become apparent as programs are examined in detail.

COMMENTS AND IMPORTANT SYMBOLS

Comments in a Pascal program are surrounded either by "(*" and "*)" or by braces (sometimes called the curly brackets). In C, comments are marked by the "/*" and "*/" characters. (Braces are used in C for other purposes, as de-

FIGURE 2.1 Outlines of typical Pascal and C programs.

Typical Pascal skeleton:

```
program ⟨name⟩ (input,output);

const
     ⟨constant declarations⟩
type
     ⟨type declarations⟩
var
     ⟨global variable declarations⟩

⟨procedures and functions⟩

begin
⟨main program body⟩
end.
```

Typical C skeleton:

```
#include ⟨stdio.h⟩
#define . . .  /* constant defns.*/
#define . . .     /* macro defns.*/

⟨global variable declarations⟩

main ()
     /*main program body*/

⟨other function definitions⟩
```

scribed below.) Figure 2.2 shows the different ways that comments are indicated in the two languages.

Other important symbols in C include the semicolon and the braces. The semicolon is used in Pascal and C for similar purposes, but there is a subtle difference. Like Pascal, C is a free-format language that leaves the exact placement of program statements on lines to the programmer. The semicolon in C is used as a statement terminator—that is, each statement must be terminated by a semicolon. This requirement is slightly different from the way that Pascal uses the semicolon as a statement separator. Thus, there will be situations in which the C programmer must use a semicolon to end a statement, whereas a Pascal programmer would not.

Braces (or curly brackets) in C are also used differently than in Pascal.

FIGURE 2.2 Comments in C and Pascal.

Pascal:

```
(* This is a comment in Pascal *)
{  So is this . . .}
```

C:

```
/* This is the only way to mark */
/* comments in C.               */
```

They can group simple statements together into a block of code often called a **compound statement**. The use of braces in C is very similar to the use of the reserved words *begin* and *end* in Pascal.

THE # SYMBOL AND THE C PREPROCESSOR

Many C programs will start off with a series of statements beginning with the symbol **#**. These lines are different from true C program statements, and they require special discussion. When C source code is compiled, the C compiler is called. Before actual compilation, however, the source code is scanned by a special program called the **C preprocessor**. The C preprocessor, which is explained in more detail in Appendix 2, interprets the lines that begin with the **#** symbol and takes appropriate action. Note that these lines do not end with semicolons.

The #include Statement

The # symbol may be followed by one of several terms, such as *include* or *define*. The **#include** statement causes external files to be included with the program code being compiled. In most C programming environments, a number of functions are available in external files to handle a variety of tasks (notably input and output). A C programmer can include any of these external files into a given source code file by using the **#include** statement.

The C skeleton in Figure 2.1 begins with the line '#include ⟨stdio.h⟩", and most C programs will begin with this line. *Note again that this line does not terminate with a semicolon, since it is not a true C program statement.* In this case, "#include ⟨stdio.h⟩" causes the file containing the input-output routines from C's standard library to be included with the program. Input and output are not intrinsically a part of the C language, a significant difference from

Pascal. No intrinsic analog exists in C for the "read" and "write" statements in Pascal. The "#include ⟨stdio.h⟩" statement adds the standard I/O routines to the program code being compiled and makes more convenient input and output possible.

The #define Statement

A second use of the C preprocessor is shown by the next few lines of the C skeleton. The **#define** statement is used to define macros, which in their simplest form are like Pascal constants. A simple definition might be "#define SIZE 50". Including this preprocessor statement will cause every occurrence of "SIZE" to be replaced by "50" before the program is compiled. As with using Pascal constants, this technique prevents burying "magic numbers" within the program and replaces them with meaningful identifiers. It also makes the program easier to modify; if a constant is used several times within a program, a single change in the **#define** statement will substitute a new value for the constant throughout the program.

VARIABLE DECLARATIONS

Variable type declarations in C are handled in a straightforward way. C has only three basic data types: **int**, **float**, and **char**. There is no predefined boolean type. Int variables store integer values, and char variables store single character values. Int variables can also be declared to be **short**, **long**, or **unsigned**; depending on the specific machine in use, "short int" or "long int" may refer to integer values of specific lengths. "Unsigned int" variables always have positive values. Float variables store single-precision real values. (In some implementations **double** variables may be available to store double-precision real values.) A more detailed discussion of C data types will be presented in Chapter 3.

The syntax used for declaring variable types is similar to that used in Pascal (see Figure 2.3). All global variables are declared in the header of the program, before any functions are defined. Local variables in Pascal are declared within the header of the individual procedures and functions, and similar variable type declarations in C are included within the header of each function definition.

There are differences, however, in handling global variables. A variable that is defined in the header of a Pascal program is global and can be referenced by any code throughout the program. In C, the scoping rules are similar, but referencing global variables within a procedure may sometimes require the global variable to be designated within the procedure as an "external" variable (Figure 2.4). C permits separate compilation and linking of program functions; if a global variable has been defined in a source file different from the code file in which it is referenced, an "extern" declaration for that variable

FIGURE 2.3 Global variable declarations in Pascal and C.

```
Pascal global variable declarations:

    <header code>
    var
        a : integer;
        b : real;
        c : boolean;
        d : char;
    <procedures, functions, main code>

C global variable type declarations:

    <header code>
    int a;
    float b;
    int c;
    char d;
    <function definitions>
```

FIGURE 2.4 Referencing global variables in Pascal and C.

```
Pascal global and local variables:
    program vardemo (input,output);
    var
        a : integer;                        (* global var *)

    function demo : real;
    var b,c : integer;                      (* local vars*)
    begin
        b := a;                   (*reference global var*)
        <rest of function code>
end;

C global and local variables:
    <header code>
    int a;                                  /* global var */

    demo ()                       /*function defn.head*/
        {                      /*equiv to Pascal 'begin'*/
        int b,c;                            /*local vars*/
        b = a;                    /*reference global var*/
        <rest of function code>
        }                      /*equiv to Pascal 'end'   */
```

is required. If the function that calls the global variable is in the same source file in which the variable was defined, then the "extern" declaration is optional.

SUBPROGRAM DEFINITIONS: FUNCTIONS AND PROCEDURES

A Pascal program consists of header code (containing type declarations, constant declarations, etc.), procedure and function definitions, and the main program code. A C program, on the other hand, has only header code (containing **#include** statements, **#define** statements, and variable type declarations) and a series of function definitions. C has no procedures, only functions. C functions may take zero or more arguments, and they may or may not return a value. C functions may occur in any order; there are fewer constraints than in Pascal. If a function returns an integer value (as most do), it may be placed anywhere in the source file, either above or below the place where it is called.

There are, of course, complications. If the function returns a value other than an integer, it should be declared before being called; this is similar to the use of **forward** *in Pascal. If a function in another file is called, it should also be declared before being called. Declaring functions will be considered in Chapter 8.*

C function definitions resemble function definitions in Pascal (Figure 2.5). The header line in the function definition contains the function name, the type of the value it returns, and the parameter list. *If the C function has no parameters, empty parentheses must still follow the function name.* C also requires that the parameter type declarations be separate from the parameter list and that the variable-type declarations be enclosed within braces, equivalent to Pascal's **begin** and **end**.

Values may be returned from C functions either via the parameter list or via the **return** statement. Returning values via the parameter list is more difficult than in Pascal. In Pascal, one need only insert the word *var* in front of the parameter to effect a change in the original argument passed in. When a function is called in C, the values of the arguments of the calling function are passed to the called function's corresponding parameters. When the called function alters these parameters within the function, the original variables remain unchanged. Changing the value of the original variables in the calling function's argument list requires passing the addresses of the arguments; this will be discussed in more detail in Chapter 8.

In C, a value for the function may also be returned via the **return** statement. The **return** statement generates a value that is returned for the function name. The function can return a value of any type. The default type of the value is **int**, but any type can be specified by defining the type immediately before the function name on the header line.

FIGURE 2.5 Outline of function definitions in Pascal and C.

Pascal function definition:

```
function ⟨name⟩ (parm1:⟨type⟩, . . . ) : ⟨type⟩;
var
     ⟨local function vars⟩ : ⟨type⟩;
begin
     ⟨function body⟩
end;
```

C function definition:

```
⟨type⟩ ⟨ functionname⟩ (parm1, parm2, . . . )
⟨parm1 type⟩ parm1;                    /*declare the parameter*/
⟨parm2 type⟩ parm2;
{                                           /*equiv of 'begin'   */
     ⟨local function vars typed⟩;
     ⟨function body⟩
     return (⟨expression⟩);
}                                               /*equiv of 'end'*/
```

THE MAIN PROGRAM CODE

In a Pascal program, the main program code is found at the end of the program, following all procedure and function definitions that might be present in the program. This main program code begins with the reserved word *begin* and ends with the reserved word *end*, followed by a period to mark the end of the program.

In a C program, the main program code is found in the function named **main** (Figure 2.6). Every complete C program must contain exactly one function named **main**. The **main** function may or may not take arguments; if arguments are specified, then their values are provided when the program is run. The **main** function need not appear at the end of the program. When the program is executed, the execution begins with the first line of the **main** function (wherever it is located), and in most ways it corresponds closely to the main program code found at the end of Pascal programs.

A SAMPLE PROGRAM

Figure 2.7 contains a short program that illustrates several of the main points made in this chapter. This short C program begins with the usual line "#include ⟨stdio.h⟩", which incorporates the standard I/O routines from the C li-

FIGURE 2.6 Outline of main program code in Pascal and C.

Pascal "main" program code:

```
(previous program code)
begin
    (main program code)
end.                                  (*end of program*)
```

C **main** program code:

```
main ( optional arguments)
(optional arguments typed)
{                                     /*equiv of 'begin'*/
    (local var declarations)
    (main program code)
}                                     /*equiv of 'end'*/
```

FIGURE 2.7 A simple C program.

```
#include <stdio.h>
#define PI 3.1416

float radius;                         /* define global var*/

main ()                               /* main function */
{                                     /* equiv to 'begin'*/
int circumference;                    /* local var*/

radius = 2.0;
circumference = 2 * PI * radius;
printf ("Hello\n");
printf("Answer is %d \n",circumference);
}                                     /*equiv to 'end' */
```

brary into the program. The constant PI is defined to have an appropriate value, and the variable "radius" is declared as a global real variable.

This short program contains only a single function, the **main** function. The **main** function has no arguments, so empty parentheses follow the function name. Braces then surround the actual function code. Within the braces, the local variable "circumference" is declared. Finally, the actual program code follows.

Notice that this program contains a statement that has not yet been mentioned. That statement is found in two lines:

```
printf ("Hello\n");
printf ("Answer is %d\n", circumference);
```

The **printf** statement is used for output in C. The details of input and output will be described in Chapter 4, but the basic syntax of **printf** can be summarized quickly. The **printf** statement takes a literal string as its first argument, followed by a list of variables. Within the literal string are various format codes, and the values of the variables are printed out according to the specifications of the format codes. The first **printf** statement in our sample program (printf ("Hello\n")) contains no variable format codes and no variables; the literal *Hello* will be the output. The second **printf** statement contains one variable format code (%d) and one variable (circumference). The format code %d causes the value of "circumference" to be printed as a decimal integer.

The **printf** statements also contain another component. At the end of the literal strings is "\n". This is one of several optional switches; the "\n" switch following the string forces a carriage-return after the string is printed. In this program, the output will be

```
Hello
The answer is ⟨circumference value⟩
```

Input and output routines will be discussed in much more detail in Chapter 5.

EXERCISES

1. Pascal provides two kinds of subprograms. Compare C and Pascal with respect to: (a) kinds of subprograms available, (b) main program code, and (c) sequence of subprograms and main program code.
2. What symbols are used to delimit comments in Pascal and C? Rewrite the following Pascal code in C.

   ```
   program firstdemo;
   {programmer: j. adams }
   {date       : 12/8/85  }
   ```

3. What does the # symbol mean in C? What does each of the following statements cause to happen?

   a. #include ⟨const.i⟩
   b. #define LIMIT 500
   c. #include ⟨stdio.h⟩

4. Given the following Pascal code, write the corresponding C code.

   a.
   ```
   var
     a : integer;
     b : integer;
   ```

```
c : real;
d : char;
```

b.
```
var
    a,b,c, : integer;
    d,e,f : real;
    g,h,i : char;
```

5. C provides no boolean data types. How could you handle boolean-like variables in C?
6. Given the following Pascal skeleton, produce the corresponding C skeleton.

```
program swapnum (input, output);
var
    firstnum : integer;
    secondnum : integer;

procedure getnumber;
begin
    ⟨procedure code⟩
end;

procedure swapnumber;
begin
    ⟨procedure code⟩
end;

procedure printresult;
begin
    ⟨procedure code⟩
end;

(* main *)
begin
    ⟨main code⟩
end.
```

CHAPTER 3

Variables and Constants in C

THE USE OF VARIABLES IN PASCAL AND C

The use of variables in C and Pascal reflects the different philosophies of the languages. Pascal programs are designed to be reliable and clear, and its use of variables reflects this. Pascal is a strongly typed language. The type of each variable must be declared before it can be used in the program, and these type declarations are made in the var-block at the head of each program, procedure, and function. Type-checking is strictly enforced throughout a Pascal program.

C, on the other hand, provides a more flexible environment for the programmer. The programmer must still declare the type of each variable before it is used, but these declarations are not set off by a distinctive reserved word such as Pascal's *var*. Instead, the declarations are simply at the head of each function or program block as required (see Figure 3.1).

Type-checking is also relaxed in C. For instance, when arguments are passed to functions, there is no type-checking for agreement between the actual parameters and the formal parameters. Data types are freely interconverted, both implicitly and explicitly using the **cast** operator (discussed below). There is no checking on array subscript range during program execution; even though an array may have been declared to have n elements, it is possible to reference the $(n+1)$*-th* element. In short, C provides an environment in which the programmer has great control. There is the potential for precise control of operations, but there is also the potential for very subtle programming errors.

FIGURE 3.1 Declaring variable types in Pascal and C.

Pascal:

```
var
     a : integer;
     b : real;
     c : char;
     d,e : integer;
     f : array [1. .50] of integer;
     g : array [1. .10] of array [1. .5] of integer;
```

C:

```
int a;
float b;
char c;
int d,e;
int f[50];
int g [10][5];
```

DECLARING AND INITIALIZING VARIABLES IN C

Legal variable names in C begin with a letter and are followed by a combination of letters and digits. The number of significant characters in a name is compiler dependent, although standard C specifies that the first eight characters are significant. Variable names may also include the underscore character, whose use is usually encouraged to increase the readability of variable names. The creative use of upper- and lowercase is also encouraged; most C compilers are case sensitive and will distinguish between uppercase and lowercase letters.

Each variable in a C program must be declared prior to its use. To declare a variable type, the following syntax is required:

⟨type⟩ ⟨var 1⟩, ⟨var 2⟩, . . . ⟨var n⟩;

Each variable declaration line consists of a type, followed by a list of one or more variable names, with the list terminated by a semicolon. Figure 3.2 shows you how C variables are typically declared.

When variables are declared in C, they may also be set to initial values at the same time. Initializing variables is a convenience not found in standard Pascal, but its use in C is common. For example, the declaration

```
int i = 0;
```

FIGURE 3.2 Sample program illustrating declaration and use of variables in C.

```
#include <stdio.h>
/* this is a remark */
/* remarks are surrounded by asterisk-slash */

/*global variable declarations */
int firstnumber;
int secondnumber, sum;

/* main program: get two numbers and add */
main ()
{
     firstnumber = 3;
     secondnumber = 4;
     sum = firstnumber + secondnumber;

     printf ("Sum of %d and %d is %d\n", firstnumber, secondnumber, sum);
}
```

both states that the variable "i" is an integer variable and sets it to the initial value 0.

Declaring and Initializing Arrays

Arrays in C are declared by entering the name of the array, followed by a dimension value surrounded by square brackets. Note that in Pascal, the programmer controls the starting and terminating index value for the array. In C, only the dimension value is declared; all arrays begin with the index value equal to zero. For instance, the declaration

```
int demoarray [5];
```

declares an array consisting of demoarray [0], demoarray [1], demoarray [2], demoarray [3], and demoarray [4]. Figure 3.1 includes an example of an array declaration.

When an array is declared in C, it may also be initialized at the same time. For example, the declaration

```
int data [5] = {2,4,6,8,10};
```

declares that the array named "data" will store five integer values, but it also initializes that array with five starting values.

Multidimensional arrays are also possible in C. A two-dimensional array could be declared by stating

```
int newarray [2] [3];
```

which declares an array of two elements by three elements. The specific array elements created by this declaration would be newarray [0] [0], newarray [0] [1], newarray [0] [2], newarray [1] [0], newarray [1] [1], and newarray [1] [2].

Multidimensional arrays can also be initialized to values at the time of declaration. For instance, the variable declaration

```
int newarray [2] [3] = { { 5, 4, 3},
                         { 9, 8, 7} };
```

initializes the array to the following values:

newarray [0] [0] → 5
newarray [0] [1] → 4
newarray [0] [2] → 3
newarray [1] [0] → 9
newarray [1] [1] → 8
newarray [1] [2] → 7

Assignment of values to multidimensional arrays is made in the usual way. The statement

```
newarray [1] [0] = 15;
```

assigns the value 15 to that array element.

Sometimes the dimension value is omitted when an array is declared. When arrays are declared as parameters being passed into a function, the dimension value is left undeclared. For example, consider the following function declaration:

```
demofunction (datarray)
int datarray [];
```

In this function, the parameter "datarray" will be given a value when the function is called, much as parameters are used in Pascal. The actual dimension of the parameter will be determined at the time of the function call, so the dimension is not declared in the function definition. Note that this convention is quite different from Pascal.

STRINGS IN C AND PASCAL

In Pascal, strings are considered arrays of characters, and the same is true in C. In C, a string can be declared following the usual declaration format:

```
char ⟨stringname⟩ [⟨dimension⟩];
```

For example, the declaration "char name [20]" declares a string with twenty possible characters. Strings in C are actually treated as constants and often are called **string constants**. A string constant in C can be defined as a one-dimensional array of characters, presented inside double quotes and terminated by the special null character, "\0". This null character can be very useful, since it can be used as an end-of-line marker. It also means that arrays representing string constants must be considered to be one character larger than the number of printing characters; one space is taken by the final null character.

String constants in C can be assigned values either by assignment statements or by initializing them to some value. For instance, the declaration

```
char message[20] = "Hello out there"
```

declares the string and initializes it to the message. Once assigned a value, the string can be manipulated in the same way that an array can be manipulated.

CONSTANT DECLARATIONS IN C

In Pascal, constants are declared in their own const-declaration block of code. The equivalent function in C can be performed with **#define** statements.

A Pascal constant is defined in the const-declaration block, in which a value that will remain unchanged throughout the program is assigned to a constant name. The use of mnemonic constant names permits self-documenting code. It also permits the programmer to make global changes during program development. By making a single alteration in the const-declaration block, a programmer can change the value of the constant throughout the program.

In a similar way, the C programmer can assign a value to a symbolic constant using the **#define** declaration. The **#define** statement is processed by the C preprocessor during program compilation and assigns the specified value to the declared constant. Constant declarations in Pascal and C are compared in Figure 3.3.

By convention, constants in C are often written in uppercase characters

FIGURE 3.3 Defining symbolic constants in Pascal and C.

Pascal:

```
const
    LIMIT = 1000;
    LOW = 0;
    HIGH = 255;
```

C:

```
#define LIMIT 100
#define LOW 0
#define HIGH 255
```

whereas variables are written in lowercase characters. This difference makes it easy to distinguish constants from variables in the program text.

DATA TYPES IN PASCAL AND C

Pascal provides a basic set of data types and a mechanism for the declaration of additional programmer-defined types. C has a much more limited range of data types. This limitation probably reflects C's roots in the language BCPL and the desire to keep the language as simple as possible yet powerful enough to build complex applications.

Pascal has four basic data types: integer, real, char, and boolean. In addition, the type-declaration block in Pascal provides the programmer with the opportunity to define new scalar types. New types are defined by listing within the type-declaration block the possible values for variables of the newly specified type (Figure 3.4). In addition, Pascal permits the definition of subrange types, a type that has permissible values associated with it which are a subset of some previously defined type.

C has three basic data types: int, float, and char. Aside from these basic types, there are additional machine-dependent types. In addition to the standard int type, short int, long int, and unsigned int may be available. In addition to the standard float type for real values, the double type may be available for additional precision. The use and precision of these types will be implementation-dependent and will vary from machine to machine.

C also provides the **typedef** declaration as an option, which looks at first glance like the type declaration in Pascal. However, these two are very different. The **typedef** declaration in C does not provide for the definition of new types—instead, it permits the programmer to create synonyms for the basic C data types. For instance, the **typedef** declaration

```
typedef int KILOGRAMS;
typedef float GRAMS, CENTIMETERS;
```

declare that the term KILOGRAMS is now synonymous with int, and that the terms GRAMS and CENTIMETERS are synonymous with float. These terms can now be used throughout the program in variable-type declarations and will increase program readability. The **typedef** declaration is usually found at the head of the program text.

The use of the Pascal type declaration and the C **typedef** declaration is illustrated in Figure 3.4.

SCOPE RULES IN PASCAL AND C

The scope of a variable is the area in a program within which the variable is known. In both C and Pascal variables have defined scopes. Some variables may be **global** in scope, and they are known throughout the program. A global variable can be referenced and changed in value throughout the program. Other variables may have more limited scope; these are **local** variables.

FIGURE 3.4 Use of the Pascal ***type*** *block and the C* ***typedef*** *statement.*

Pascal type declarations:

```
type
     string = array[1. .20] of char;
     lines = array[1. .10] of string;
```

C:

```
typedef int METERS;
typedef float KILOMETERS;
```

(NOTE: The C **typedef** statement only creates synonyms for existing types; it does not define new types.)

In Pascal, a variable is known at the level of program organization at which it is defined and at all lower levels. For instance, a variable defined at the **program** level is global and known within all functions and procedures in the program. If it is defined within a procedure or function, its scope is local and it is known only within that procedure or function and any procedures defined (or nested) within that procedure or function.

Variables in C may also be global or local in scope. To define a global variable, the C programmer declares a variable at the head of the program text, outside of any function code so that all functions in the source file can access that variable (see Figure 3.5).

C programs can be constructed from functions written in separate files and linked during compilation into a single program. If a global variable in one file must be accessed by a function in another file, then the variable must also be declared in the second file and the declaration line must begin with the reserved word extern. *This declaration establishes that the variable already exists and is external to this file.*

If a C variable is defined within a function, its scope is local and it is known only within that function (see Figure 3.6). In Pascal a local variable may be defined within a procedure; it may then still be known to other procedures that are defined (nested) within the main procedure. Functions in C cannot be defined (or nested) within other functions, so there is no similar situation in C.

STORAGE CLASSES FOR VARIABLES IN C

The variable-type declaration line in C programs may contain more information than just the variable name and the basic data type associated with it.

27 *FIGURE 3.5 Schematic view of access to global variables in C.*

28

```
#include <stdio.h>
   int a;
```

29

```
main()
{
     <main code>
}
```

30

```
function1 ( . . .
{
     <function code>
}
```

31

```
function2 ( . . .
{
     <function code>
}
```

32

FIGURE 3.6 Schematic view of access to local variables in C.

```
#include <stdio.h>
int a;

main()
{
     int b;
        <main code>
}

function1 ( . . .
{
     int c;
        <function code>
}
```

The declaration line may also specify information about how the variable is to be stored, how permanent it will be, and which parts of the program will have access to it. The programmer may thus supply what is called **storage class** information about the variable.

There are four possible storage classes available in C: the first is the **extern** variable declaration, by which a variable is made available to several component files that make up the program. For instance, if the variable named "globalvar" has been declared in one source file, and a function in a second source file must use it, then the appropriate declarations might be

File 1:

```
#include <stdio.h>
int globalvar;
    ⟨rest of File 1⟩
```

File 2:

```
#include <stdio.h>
extern int globalvar;
    ⟨rest of File 2⟩
```

This use of **extern** will make the variable "globalvar" defined in File 1 available to functions in File 2.

The other possible storage classes for variables are **automatic**, **static**, and **register**. These storage classes can be specified for any variable by adding appropriate information to the variable-type declaration line, just as for **extern** variables. However, only one storage-class specifier may be added to a variable's type declaration. The following sections will explain briefly these possible storage classes.

SAVING LOCAL VALUES—AUTOMATIC AND STATIC VARIABLES

In Pascal, variable values can be accessed and changed in several different ways. A global variable can be accessed and its value changed throughout the program. A local variable that is declared within a procedure is created each time the procedure is called. (Variables that are procedure or function arguments present a more complicated situation, and we will defer consideration of arguments until Chapter 8.)

A C programmer has more control over this process. As we have seen, global variables can be created easily. Local variables can be created by declaring variables within functions. In addition to these Pascal-like features, the C programmer also controls whether local variables retain their values between function calls. In Pascal, a local variable is created anew each time a procedure is called, and the values from previous procedure calls are not retained. If the C programmer takes no action, the same situation is true. Local variables will be recreated each time a function is called, and variable values from previous calls to that function will not be retained. Under this default situation, variables are said to be **automatic**.

A variable can, however, be declared to be **static**. A static variable within a function is a local variable that retains its values from previous calls to that function. They are created the first time that the function is called and are not destroyed when the function is exited. A static local variable is declared by using the following format within the variable-type declaration line:

static ⟨variable type⟩ ⟨variable name⟩;

Global variables can also be declared to be static, but this has a different meaning. Remember that global variables are declared outside of any function, usually at the head of the program text, and can be accessed through an **extern** declaration by any function in any file linked together during compilation. If a global variable is declared static, however, it can be accessed only by functions physically located within that file, not by functions in the other files that may be contributing to the program.

The use of static external variables lets the C programmer share variables within a group of functions in one file. Two different files can also use static external variables of the same name without any conflict, because the static external variables in one file will be unknown and inaccessible to the other file. The use of static external variables provides a scope that is somewhat more than local but less than truly global.

REGISTER VARIABLES IN C

So far we have discussed the use of external variables, automatic variables, and static variables. These examples of storage classes define possible properties that may be associated with C variables.

There is a fourth possible storage class for C variables. If a variable will be referenced often, it can be declared as a **register** variable. If possible, the host machine will store that variable in a machine register and permit faster access during program execution. The actual implementation of register variables is obviously machine dependent, since the number of available registers will vary. In general, if no registers are available, the register variable declaration will be ignored. The declaration of a register variable requires the following syntax:

register ⟨variable type⟩ ⟨variable name⟩;

INITIALIZING VARIABLES IN PASCAL AND C

Pascal variables must always be assigned a value before being referenced. Failure to initialize a variable before referencing it will result in an error. In

UCSD Pascal, the uninitialized variable will start off with a random, meaningless value, which can produce a very subtle program bug.

Failure to initialize a variable in C will not result in an error message. *This is another case in which C compilers assume that the programmer is in control and knows what he or she is doing.* Static and external variables that are not initialized will begin with the value of zero. Automatic and register variables that are not initialized will have unpredictable values. Since most variables in C are local automatic variables, the programmer must take care to initialize variables so they will have specific initial values.

TYPE CONVERSIONS AND THE CAST OPERATION

In a C program, type conversions can be accomplished by using the **cast** operation. The cast operation explicitly converts (or casts) the value of a variable into a type that is different from the original type of the variable.

This operation is performed by preceding a variable name by the new type. For example, if *x* is originally declared to be type int and *y* is declared to be type float, the statement

```
y = (float) x;
```

will convert the integer value of *x* to its corresponding float value and assign that value to *y*. *Note: This conversion does not change the value or the type of x.*

In addition to the cast operation, automatic type conversion can also occur in the execution of some expressions. For instance, if *x* is type int and *z* is type float, then the result of the expression $(x + z)$ will be of type float; that is, the value of *x* is promoted to type float before the operation is carried out. In mixed arithmetic operations, the values of int variables are automatically promoted to float.

There is also a special case involving automatic type conversions that deserves mention. When variables of type int are mixed in expressions with variables of type char, then the result is type int. There are special situations involving text manipulation when this conversion is useful.

UNIONS IN C

Some programs may include special situations in which a variable must store one data type under certain circumstances and another data type under other circumstances. (Remember that similar situations might be handled in Pascal using variant records.) C provides a special mechanism—the **union**—for handling these situations.

A union permits a single variable in C to store data of several different types. It is declared using the following general syntax:

```
union <union-tag>
    { <type> <member name>;
      <type> <member name>;
      <continue until all alternative types are specified>
    } <variable name>;
```

This declaration has several components. First, the word *union* must precede the declaration. Second, a "union-tag" must be specified; this is any legal identifier that identifies the type of union being defined. *This union-tag can be used later in the program if necessary for declaring other variables to have this same basic structure.* Third, the alternative types that can be stored by the variable are declared; each of these is on a separate line, along with an identifier (the "member name") that will permit access to that type later. Last, there is the name of the specific variable that is being declared to be a union. The following is an example of a union declaration:

```
union demouniontype
    { int a;
      float b;
    } demovariable;
```

In this example, the variable "demovariable" is declared as a union that can store either int or float values. The identifiers "a" and "b" specify the members of the union and provide the means by which the different data types can be accessed. To store or access either data type, the following statements could be used:

```
    demovariable.a = 1;
or
    demovariable.b = 4.6;
```

One thing to remember about unions is that although a variable declared as a union can store several different data types, it can store only one data type at a time. It is easy to get the impression, for instance, that "demovariable" in our example can store both int and float values at the same time, like the fields of a record in Pascal, but this is not true. A union can store only one of the alternative data types at a time.

EXERCISES

1. List the four basic data types available in C and the corresponding types in Pascal.
2. Given the following Pascal code, write the corresponding C code:

```
const
    LIMIT = 100;
var
    grade : char;
```

```
score : integer;
name : array [1. .20] of char;
```

3. In the following C variable declaration, give the array name, number of memory cells reserved, and the index values of all cells.

```
int scores [5];
```

What would happen if a program statement read a value from the tenth element in the array?

4. Explain the use of **typedef** in C. How is this declaration similar to and different from type definitions in Pascal?
5. Explain the differences between global variables in Pascal and the **extern** storage class in C. Why does C need the **extern** declaration but Pascal doesn't?
6. Explain the difference between the **automatic** and **static** storage classes. Does Pascal provide a way for creating the equivalent of the **static** storage class?
7. Examine the following C code. Is it correct? If not, why not? Explain what its output would be.

```
#include <stdio.h>
int a;
main ()
    { a = a*a;
      printf ("Value of a is %d\n",a);
    }
```

CHAPTER 4

Operations in C and Pascal

ARITHMETIC OPERATORS IN C

Pascal and C provide similar arithmetic operators, a summary of which is presented in Figure 4.1. Both Pascal and C provide the familiar +, −, *, and / binary arithmetic operators, and the precedence rules are identical. The * and / operators have the highest priority, with the + and − operators having lower precedence.

Both languages also provide a **modulus** operator. In Pascal, the expression "a mod b" (where a and b are integers) returns the remainder from the operation a divided by b. In C, the modulus operator is "%"; the above expression in C would be "a % b". There is no C equivalent for the Pascal **div** operator. *However, the division operator "/" in C can behave like the Pascal* **div** *operator if both its arguments are type int.*

FIGURE 4.1 Arithmetic operators in Pascal and C.

Operation	Pascal	C
Addition	+	+
Subtraction	−	−
Multiplication	*	*
Division	/	/
Mod	mod	%
Div	div	

RELATIONAL OPERATORS

C and Pascal also have similar relational operators, which are summarized in Figure 4.2. Both languages use the familiar algebraic symbols <, < =, >, and > = to mean "less than," "less than or equal to," "greater than," and "greater than or equal to."

The equality and inequality operators are slightly different, and this difference is related to the assignment operator used in the two languages. In Pascal, the assignment operator is the ": = " symbol; the assignment statement "a := 4;" assigns the value 4 to the variable a. The " = " symbol is used as the equality operator in Pascal; the statement "if a = 4" tests to see if a is equal to 4. The inequality operator in Pascal is "<>"; the statement "if a <> 4" tests to see if a is not equal to 4.

C uses different symbols for these operations. The " = " symbol is used for assignment; thus, the statement "a = 4" assigns the value 4 to the variable a. The equality operator in C is " = = ", which means the statement "if (a = = 4)" tests to see if a is equal to 4. The inequality operator is "! = ", and the statement "if (a != 4)" tests to see if a is not equal to 4.

LOGICAL OPERATORS

Logical operations in C and Pascal are similar, but the actual operators used are quite different. The logical operators are summarized in Figure 4.3.

The negation operator in Pascal is the word *not*; in the statement "if (not found)", the negation operator will negate the logical value of a boolean variable called "found." The negation operator in C is the "!" symbol. *Thus, the inequality operator "!= " can literally be read as "not equal."* The same expression in C would be "if (! found)".

The logical connective "and" in Pascal is represented in C by the "&&" symbol. Thus, the Pascal statement "if (a = 4) and (b = 5)" would be written in C as "if (a = = 4) && (b= = 5)".

The logical connective "or" in Pascal is represented in C by the "||" symbol. Thus, the Pascal statement "if (d = 6) or (e = 7)" would be written in C as "if (d = = 6) || (e = =7)".

Under standard C syntax, the evaluation of logical "and" and "or" expressions proceeds somewhat differently than it does in Pascal. In C, the elements of these logical expressions are evaluated only until the value of the entire expression can be determined. For example, if the lefthand component of a logical "and" evaluates to "false," then the righthand component need not be evaluated, and the expression as a whole evaluates to "false." Likewise, if the lefthand component of an "or" expression evaluates to "true," then the righthand component is not evaluated, and the expression as a whole evaluates to "true." This procedure is different from the implementation of most Pascal compilers, in which the entire expression is evaluated regardless of whether the value of the expression can be determined by partial evaluation.

FIGURE 4.2 Relational operators in Pascal and C.

Relational Operation	Pascal	C
Greater than	>	>
Greater than or equal	>=	>=
Less than	<	<
Less than or equal	<=	<=
Not equal	<>	!=
Equality	=	==

FIGURE 4.3 Logical operators in Pascal and C.

	Pascal	C
Negation operator	not	!
Logical and	and	&&
Logical or	or	||

SPECIAL C OPERATORS: INCREMENT AND DECREMENT OPS

In addition to the usual arithmetic, relational, and logical operators, C provides several operators not found in Pascal. These are outlined in Figure 4.4.

Two of these operators are used to increment and decrement variables. The "++" operator is used to increment variables. The statement "++ ⟨variable name⟩" increments the value of the variable by 1. The "--" operator is used to decrement variable values. The statement "-- ⟨variable name⟩" subtracts 1 from the value of the variable named. These operators replace the rather clumsy statements used in other languages to increment or decrement variable values. Thus, the Pascal statements

```
firstvariable := firstvariable + 1;
secondvariable := secondvariable - 1;
```

could be written in C as

```
++firstvariable;
--secondvariable;
```

FIGURE 4.4 Use of C increment and decrement ops.

The C increment operator:

+ + ⟨variable name⟩;
⟨variable name⟩ + +;

The C decrement operator:

− − ⟨variable name⟩;
⟨variable name⟩ − −;

These increment and decrement operators have additional properties. They can be used as either prefix or postfix operators; for instance, the increment operation described above may also be written as "firstvariable + + ". In many situations, the effect of both notations will be the same.

In some situations, however, the effects of using the prefix or the postfix notation will be quite different. The prefix notation means "increment the value of the variable, and then use the value," whereas the postfix notation means "use the current value of the variable, and then increment it." This distinction is important in any program code in which the increment or decrement operation is part of a larger expression, a common occurrence in C programs. For instance, the program statement

```
firstvariable = + + secondvariable;
```

is very different from the statement

```
firstvariable = secondvariable + +;
```

In both statements, the value of secondvariable is incremented by 1, but the value of firstvariable will be different in the two statements. In the first statement, firstvariable is assigned the incremented value of secondvariable—in the prefix notation, the variable is incremented and then the new value of the variable is used. In the second version, however, firstvariable is assigned the old value of secondvariable, and then secondvariable is incremented; that is, in the postfix notation, the current value of the variable is used and then the variable is incremented.

SPECIAL C OPERATORS: BITWISE OPS

In addition to the increment and decrement operators, C also provides operators for **bitwise** operations. These operators are summarized in Figure 4.5. Bit manipulation operations may be used only on type int variables.

FIGURE 4.5 Bitwise operations in C.

Operation	Operator
Bitwise and	&
Bitwise or	|
Bitwise xor	^
Bitwise shift-right	>>
Bitwise shift-left	<<
One's complement	~

These bitwise operations permit the C programmer to perform the boolean **and**, **or**, and **xor** operations. The "&" symbol is used for the bitwise **and** operation; the "|" symbol, for the bitwise **or** operation; and the "^" symbol, for bitwise **exclusive or**.

An example of the use of the logical bitwise **and** operator might be

```
firstvar = secondvar & ⟨value⟩;
```

This statement will compare—bit by bit—the bit-pattern for secondvar with the bit-pattern for the stated value. Based on the results of a logical **and** at each bit position, a new bit-pattern will be constructed and that value assigned to firstvar. Thus, if secondvar = 11 and ⟨value⟩ = 3, the value of firstvar would be calculated as:

```
secondvar ——> 0 000 000 000 001 011 (in octal)
⟨value⟩   ——> 0 000 000 000 000 011 (in octal)
-----------------------------------------------
firstvar  ——> 0 000 000 000 000 011 (——> 3)
```

In general, & operations are useful for assigning bit-patterns that match the pattern in the ⟨value⟩ used in the statement. In this example, the bits in firstvar will be set to 1 wherever the ⟨value⟩ pattern is set to 1; the other bits in the secondvar bit-pattern will be zeroed out. The ⟨value⟩ bit-pattern is an example of a **mask**, a pattern that can be used to set certain bit locations to a predetermined value.

The **or** can be used in a similar way to manipulate bit-patterns. A typical example of the use of the bitwise **or** operator is

```
thirdvar = fourthvar | ⟨value⟩;
```

In this example, the bit-patterns for fourthvar and the stated value are compared. The bit-pattern for thirdvar is constructed by performing a logical **or** bit by bit on the two patterns. So, if fourthvar = 11 and ⟨value⟩ = 5, the result would be:

```
fourthvar  ——> 0 000 000 001 011 (octal)
⟨value⟩    ——> 0 000 000 000 101 (octal)
--------------------------------------------
thirdvar   ——> 0 000 000 001 111 (——> 15)
```

In general, the bitwise **or** can be used to set to 1 in a bit-pattern the same bits that are set to 1 in the given ⟨value⟩. Once again, the ⟨value⟩ pattern is a mask that is used to set certain bit locations to a predetermined value.

In addition to bitwise logical operations, C provides other operators for direct manipulation of bit-patterns. These include the ">>" operator (which shifts the bit-pattern in a variable to the right by a specified number of positions) and the "<<" operator (which shifts the bit-pattern in a variable to the left by a specified number of positions). In general, the syntax used with these shift operators is

```
⟨var⟩ = ⟨var⟩ >> ⟨expression⟩;
⟨var⟩ = ⟨var⟩ << ⟨expression⟩;
```

where the value of the expression determines the number of positions the bit-pattern will shift to the left or to the right.

Another operator that directly manipulates bit-patterns is the unary operator "~", which takes a bit-pattern and produces the one's complement of that pattern. In other words, all the bits set to 1 in a variable will be set to 0, and all the bits set to 0 in it will be set to 1, and the new bit-pattern is assigned to the specified variable.

The following are typical examples of how these bitwise operators are used:

```
firstvar = secondvar << 2;
thirdvar = fourthvar >> 1;
fifthvar = ~ sixthvar;
```

If secondvar = 1 and this bit-pattern were shifted two positions to the left, then the value of firstvar would be 4. If fourthvar = 4 and this bit-pattern were shifted one position to the right, then the value of thirdvar would be 2. In the unary operation, fifthvar will be assigned the one's complement value of sixthvar.

CONDENSING MULTIPLE OPERATIONS IN C

C can be an extremely concise language. This is one of its attractions and one of its real problems. The nature of C permits programmers to produce short, elegant, and almost unreadable code.

One way of abbreviating C code is to combine multiple operations into a single statement. For instance, the statement

```
firstvar = firstvar * secondvar;
```

can be made more concise. The following code is exactly the same statement:

firstvar *= secondvar;

In general, any assignment statement in which the variable or expression on the left side of the statement is used again on the right side of the statement can be compressed. If the assignment statement can be reduced to the form

⟨variable⟩ = ⟨variable⟩ ⟨operation⟩ ⟨rest of statement⟩;

the statement can be rewritten as ⟨variable⟩ ⟨operation⟩ = ⟨rest of statement⟩;

PRECEDENCE OF OPERATIONS IN C

Good programming style will include the use of appropriate parentheses in expressions. This convention forces operations to be performed in the sequence desired by the programmer. In complex expressions, the order in which components are evaluated can thus be carefully controlled.

To produce very concise code, however, some programmers prefer to depend on the built-in precedence of operators and will construct expressions so that they can be evaluated correctly without the use of parentheses. For those programmers, I have summarized in Figure 4.6 the order of precedence of the operators discussed in this chapter. The operators are ranked in order of precedence; those at the top of the list have highest precedence, and operators on the same line have equal precedence. If an expression contains operators of equal precedence, then they are evaluated strictly on a left-to-right basis.

FIGURE 4.6 Precedence of operators in C.

Highest precedence

```
++, --, !, ~
*  /  %
+  -
<<, >>
==, !=
&
^
|
&&
||
=
```

Lowest precedence

EXERCISES

1. Given the following Pascal code, write the corresponding C code:

   a. a := b + c;
   b. a := b * c;
   c. a := b/c;

- **d.** a := b mod c;
- **e.** a := b div c;

If b has the initial value of 10 and c has the initial value of 3, what is the value of a in each case?

2. Write the corresponding C code for the following Pascal code.

- **a.** if (a>=b) . . .
- **b.** if (a <> b) . . .
- **c.** if ((a>b) and (c<d)) . . .
- **d.** if ((a>b) or (c>d)) . . .

3. Given the following Pascal code, write the corresponding C code:

- **a.** a := a + 1;
- **b.** a := a − 1;
- **c.** a := a * b;

4. Look at the following C code. If initially a = 2, b = 3, and c = 4, then what is the value of a after each statement?

- **a.** ++a;
- **b.** −−a;
- **c.** a *= b;
- **d.** a = b % c;

5. If a = 1, then what is the value of b after each statement?

- **a.** b = a>>1;
- **b.** b = a<<1;
- **c.** b = ~a;

6. Using the appropriate C bitwise operators, write the C statements that would:

- **a.** set any given bit-pattern to zero
- **b.** set any given bit-pattern to 1
- **c.** set any bit-pattern to its one's-complement value (in which each bit is reversed in value)
- **d.** set any bit-pattern to its two's-complement value (in which the bit-pattern is reversed and then the value 1 is added).

7. Stating any necessary assumptions about how integers are stored on your specific machine, write the appropriate C statements that will convert any bit-pattern to its:

- **a.** decimal value
- **b.** hexadecimal value
- **c.** octal value.

CHAPTER 5

Input and Output in C and Pascal

GENERAL OVERVIEW

So far we've discussed the basic structure of a C program, the basic data types provided in the language, and the operators available for use. We've also contrasted these with the structure of Pascal programs and the types and operators available in Pascal. Before moving onto a discussion of the control structures used in C and Pascal, it's important to understand a little bit about input and output in the two languages.

Pascal has been justifiably criticized for its limited input/output capabilities. The language was primarily designed to be a teaching tool, and the details of I/O on specific systems were omitted. Pascal has a very limited capability for producing formatted output, and there is no provision for reading formatted input.

C is even more limited. C was designed to be concise, and the details of input to and output from programs were not included at all in the formal language specification. Instead, it was assumed that input and output would be handled primarily by the operating system, and that system-dependent code could be written to handle the details of input and output for any specific system.

Many implementations of C run under the UNIX operating system, which has a library of functions for handling input and output. Indeed, these input/output functions are so widely available that in some sense they can be considered a near-universal extension of the language. These library functions are included into most C programs running under UNIX by using the line "#include ⟨stdio.h⟩" at the beginning of the source text. This statement is a call to the C preprocessor to add the standard I/O library functions to the source text.

An identical command line is used by many C compilers operating in other, non-UNIX environments.

The standard input/output library functions under UNIX treat input and output as if they were streams of characters. The source of the input stream is called **standard input**, and the place to which the output stream is directed is called **standard output**. The default value for standard input is generally the keyboard, and the default value for standard output is the terminal screen, although these defaults may vary among installations. Under UNIX, it is easy to alter standard input and output from the default value to any convenient file or device. (This will be discussed in Chapter 10.)

There are a number of input/output routines in the library file, but we will concentrate on the most useful ones: **printf**, **scanf**, **putchar**, and **getchar**.

PASCAL'S WRITE AND C'S PRINTF

The **write** and **writeln** commands in Pascal are the most commonly used output commands in that language. The **write** command is followed by a list of arguments inside parentheses. This list can contain any combination of literal strings (enclosed in single quotation marks) and variable names, each separated by commas. The **write** command will print out the values associated with the argument list. The **writeln** command will print the values of the list and will also print a carriage return and line feed at the end of the list, thus forcing the next output to begin on a new line. Figure 5.1 provides a quick review of the **write** and **writeln** statements.

Pascal provides limited control over the format of output. The names of variables on the argument list can be followed by various specifications that control the width of the field to be used when printing out values and the number of values to the right of the decimal point to be displayed when printing real values. For instance, the statement

```
write (var1:10, var2:10:3);
```

prints the value of var1 right-justified in an output field ten characters wide, and then prints the value of var2 right-justified in a field ten characters wide, with three numbers displayed to the right of the decimal point.

Most C environments provide a function that gives the C programmer the same kind of control over output. The **printf** function in the C standard input/output library is probably one of the most commonly used C functions. It serves the same basic purpose as the **write** or **writeln** command in Pascal, but it also allows considerably greater control over the format of the output.

The syntax associated with the **printf** function is superficially similar to that of the Pascal **write** command. Figure 5.2 lists the C equivalent of the Pascal output statements in Figure 5.1. Note the similarities and differences.

FIGURE 5.1 Uses of the **write** *and* **writeln** *statements in Pascal.*

Statement:	write ('⟨literal string⟩');
Effect:	Output the literal string.
Statement:	writeln ('⟨literal string⟩');
Effect:	Output literal string, followed by a newline.
Statement:	write ('⟨literal string⟩',⟨var1⟩);
Effect:	Output literal string, followed by value of var1.
Statement:	write ('⟨literal string⟩',⟨var1⟩:n);
Effect:	Output literal string, followed by value of var1 right-justified in field n characters wide.
Statement:	write ('⟨literal string⟩', ⟨var1⟩:n:m);
Effect:	Output literal string, followed by value of real variable var1 in field n characters wide with m digits to right of the decimal point.

FIGURE 5.2 Use of the **printf** *statement in C.*

Statement:	printf ("⟨literal string⟩");
Effect:	Output the literal string.
Statement:	printf ("⟨literal string⟩\n");
Effect:	Output the literal string, followed by a newline.
Statement:	printf("⟨string. . .%d. . .⟩",⟨var1⟩);
Effect:	Output string with value of var1 printed as decimal integer at position marked by %d.
Statement:	printf("⟨string. . .%nd. .⟩",⟨var1⟩);
Effect:	Output string with value of var1 printed at position marked by %d, right-justified in field n characters wide.
Statement:	printf("⟨string. . .%n.pf. .",⟨var1⟩);
Effect:	Output string with value of real var1 printed in field n characters wide, with precision p.

The function name **printf** is followed by an argument list, but the argument list is organized very differently from the list in Pascal.

The simplest use of the **printf** statement would be to print out a literal string that includes no variable values. The general format for such a statement would be:

```
printf ("<literal string>");
```

The format of this statement is very similar to the related **writeln** statement.

Differences are seen, however, when we consider printing out a literal string with variable values imbedded within it. In Pascal, the variable names are listed on the argument list at the point where the value is to be printed:

```
writeln ( '<literal>',<var1>, '<literal>', <var2>, etc.);
```

In C, the literal string is the first item on the argument list, and it is followed by a list of the variables whose values will be imbedded in the string. The literal string includes a series of special characters to reserve the locations where the variable values will be printed. In general, the format used for the **printf** statement will be:

```
printf ("<literal string with special chars>", <var1>, <var2>, etc.);
```

A typical **printf** statement might look like this:

```
printf ("the sum of %d and %d is %d\n", var1, var2, var3);
```

The first element on the argument list is the control string, which (as the name implies) controls the output. The control string is enclosed by quotation marks, and the characters within the string are printed literally on the standard output—except for the characters preceded by the % symbol or the \ symbol. A list of variable names follows this control string.

Characters in the control string preceded by the backslash (\) symbol are called **escape sequences**. These escape sequences can be used to format the output or to print otherwise unprintable characters, such as the single quote. In this example, the characters "\n" will cause a carriage return and line feed after the line is printed out. The letter *n* is used to force this action, since the combination of carriage return and line feed is often called a **newline.**

Characters preceded by the % symbol are embedded within the control string to mark the place in the string in which the variables' values will be printed. The actual values that are printed will be taken from the variable list following the control string. Thus, the value of the first variable will be printed at the location of the first % symbol, the second variable's value will be printed at the location of the second %, and so on. In the example above, the output would look like this:

```
The sum of ⟨var1 value⟩ and ⟨var2 value⟩ is ⟨var3 value⟩
```

Notice that neither the % symbol nor the character following it was printed out. They were simply reserving space in the literal string for the variable values and specifying how these values were to be printed. *Variables in C are more flexible than variables in many other languages; a reference to a variable is a reference to a bit-pattern in a specific memory location—and that bit-pattern can be interpreted as different things (integer, character, etc.)*

The combination of the % symbol and the character following it is called a **conversion specification**. (Figure 5.3 summarizes the conversion specifications possible in C.) It specifies how a variable is to be converted when it is output. For instance, "%d" means to convert the variable into a decimal value and print that value. The combination "%o" means to convert the variable into an octal value and print that value. If we changed the above **printf** statement to

```
printf ("The sum of %o and %o is %o", var1, var2, var3);
```

then the output would be similar, except that the values would now be expressed in octal.

The conversion specifications in the **printf** function also provide for some control over output format. Between the % and the conversion character (d, u, o, x, etc.), it is possible to insert format information. The following examples demonstrate the most common format controls:

%nd → right-justify the output in a field *n* chars wide
%−nd → left-justify the output in a field *n* chars wide
%n.pd → left-justify in a field *n* chars wide, with precision *p*.

The meaning of **precision** *will depend on variable type. If the variable is a real number, precision will mean how many numbers to print to the right of*

FIGURE 5.3 Conversion specifications for the ***printf*** *statement in C.*

Conversion Specification	Effect
%d	decimal notation
%u	unsigned decimal notation
%o	unsigned octal notation
%x	unsigned hexadecimal notation
%e	exponential notation
%f	floating-point notation
%g	%e or %f, whichever is shorter
%c	single character
%s	string

FIGURE 5.4 Escape sequences to use in the ***printf*** *control string in C.*

Escape sequence	Effect
\n	newline
\t	tab
\r	carriage return
\f	formfeed
\b	backspace one character
\'	output the ' character
\\	output the \ character

the decimal point. If the variable is a string, precision will mean how many characters in the string to print.

In addition to conversion specifications, escape sequences also determine the output format of a **printf** statement. The character following the backslash (\) specifies format information that is used when the control string is output. We have already seen that the sequence "\n" causes a newline (a carriage return and line feed) to be output. Likewise, if the characters "\t" are embedded in the control string, then a tab is output at that point. Figure 5.4 summarizes possible escape sequences.

PASCAL'S READ AND C'S SCANF

The **read** and the related **readln** statements are Pascal input statements. The **read** statement reads values from some designated input source and assigns those values to an input list of variables. The input source may be any specified source file or a device such as the keyboard.

For instance, the Pascal statement

```
read ( ⟨var1⟩, ⟨var2⟩, ⟨var3⟩);
```

reads from some standard input source a list of values and assigns those values to ⟨var1⟩, ⟨var2⟩, and ⟨var3⟩. Under default conditions, the **read** statement reads from the system file called INPUT, which usually corresponds to the keyboard on interactive systems.

The related **readln** statement performs a similar function, reading a list of values from an input source file, and then moving the file position pointer to the beginning of the next input line in the file. *In a sense, the* **readln** *reads in the number of input values required to assign values to the variables on its* *parameter list, and then performs a carriage return. Any values remaining on the current line in the input file are skipped over, and the next input is taken from the beginning of the next line.*

The corresponding operation is performed in C by the **scanf** function, a predefined function that is part of the standard input/output library, included into a C source file by the statement "#include ⟨stdio.h⟩".

The **scanf** function closely resembles the **printf** function in format. The general format for the **scanf** statement is as follows:

```
scanf ("⟨control string⟩", arg1, arg2,. . .argn);
```

There is a control string, just as in the **printf** statement. However, this control string works a little differently. Although it also contains a set of conversion specifications, they determine how the input source file data will be interpreted. Data is read from the source file, interpreted under the control of the conversion specifications in the control string, and then assigned to the corresponding variable on the argument list. *The* **scanf** *statement resembles the* **format** *statement used in FORTRAN for formatted input.*

A summary of the conversion specifications available for use with the **scanf** statement is provided in Figure 5.5. This list is very similar to the list of conversion specifications presented for use in **printf** statements, and they are used in similar ways.

A complication that makes use of the **scanf** statement somewhat clumsy is that the argument list must not include a simple list of variables to be assigned values. Instead, the argument list consists of a list of pointers to the variables to be assigned values. (Pointers will be discussed in Chapter 9.)

The following is a typical **scanf** statement:

```
scanf ("%f %d %4d", &⟨var1⟩, &⟨var2⟩, &⟨var3⟩);
```

FIGURE 5.5 Input conversion specifications in the **scanf** *statement.*

Conversion Specifications	Meaning
%d	decimal integer expected
%o	octal integer expected
%x	hexadecimal integer expected
%h	short integer expected
%c	character expected
%s	string expected
%f	real value expected
%e	real value expected (exponential notation)

The first conversion specification, %f, means to read the input line and assign the first value to the variable ⟨var1⟩ as a real value. *The & preceding ⟨var1⟩'s name indicates that you are working with a pointer to the variable.* The second conversion specification, %d, means to interpret the next value on the input line as a decimal integer and assign it to ⟨var2⟩. The third conversion specification, %4d, contains a field width specifier in addition to a type specifier; this instruction means to read only the first four digits of the next value and assign them as a decimal integer value to ⟨var3⟩.

The operations performed by the **scanf** function are relatively high level. Many of the same operations can be performed at a lower level by the **getchar** and **getc** functions, two C primitive input functions described in the next section.

I/O PRIMITIVES IN PASCAL AND C

Most Pascal and C environments provide for the limited input and output capabilities described in the previous sections. In addition, many environments for both languages provide the programmer with more primitive operations.

In Pascal, the **put** and **get** commands provide control over a file buffer variable. The **get** command is an input command that reads the next element from a file and stores it in a file buffer variable. The file position pointer within the file is not advanced. This makes it possible to examine the next element of a file before using a **read** statement to actually read the element and advance the file position pointer.

The **put** command is the corresponding output command that writes the current contents of the file buffer variable to the end of the output file. Figure 5.6 provides a schematic view of how **get** and **put** operate in Pascal.

C also provides more primitive operations than **printf** and **scanf**. These are the related functions **getchar**, **getc**, **putchar**, and **putc**. *Actually, these may be implemented alternatively as either functions or macros within the standard input/output library.*

The **getchar** function in C gets the next character from the standard input and returns it as the function's value. For example, if the variable "c" is of type character, then the statement

```
c = getchar();
```

would result in the next character in the standard input stream being assigned to the variable "c."

In a similar way, the **putchar** function outputs a single character to standard output. If "c" is of type character, then the statement

```
putchar (c);
```

will print out the variable "c" on standard output.

The **getc** and **putc** functions (or macros) permit you to get single charac-

FIGURE 5.6 Schematic view of the ***get*** *and* ***put*** *commands in Pascal.*

INITIAL SITUATION

INPUT STREAM:
⟨char1⟩⟨char2⟩⟨char3⟩⟨char4⟩⟨char5⟩. . .

↑___ initial position
of input file pointer

OUTPUT STREAM:
⟨lastchar⟩⟨end-of-file⟩

↑___ initial position
of output file pointer

1. Effect of **get** command: read the value of ⟨char2⟩ into a buffer variable, but do not advance the file pointer. If desired, this can be followed by a READ command, which will read the value of ⟨char2⟩ into a variable and also advance the file pointer.

2. Effect of **put** command: take the value of a buffer variable, place it after ⟨lastchar⟩ on the output stream, and adjust the file pointer to point to the new terminal character.

ters or output single characters to files other than standard input or output. These functions take file specifiers as arguments, but otherwise they are very similar to the **getchar** and **putchar** functions. (The use of **getc** and **putc** will be discussed in more detail in Chapter 10.) Figure 5.7 outlines the operation of these I/O primitives.

SOFTWARE C TOOLS: COPYING TEXT

The concept of software tools is common in the C community. A **tool** is a general-use program that performs a simple task and that can be linked to other similar tools to perform increasingly complex tasks. *The concept is presented in detail in the elegant book "Software Tools," by Brian Kernighan and P. J.* Plauger.

Throughout the rest of this book we will develop a few simple tools to illustrate the use of C in practical programs. The first such tool is presented in Figure 5.8. This program is simple but serves its purpose efficiently. Using the C I/O primitives **getc** and **putchar**, the contents of a file are displayed on the standard output.

FIGURE 5.7 Typical character input and output in C.

```
char c;

/* get character from standard input*/
c = getchar();

/* write to standard output */
putchar(c);

/* get character from some file */
/* specified by file pointer fd    */
c = getc (fd);

/* write to file specified by      */
/* file pointer fd2                */
putc ( c, fd2);
```

FIGURE 5.8 Program "filedisplay.c" gets the contents of a file named "low.c" and displays it on the standard output. (Note: The file "low.c" is specified using the special file specification required by a CP/M compiler. Consult your system manuals for the details of use of the function **getc** *on your system.)*

```
#include <stdio.h>
char c;
main ()
{
  while (c != EOF)
    { c = getc ("O/A: low.c ");
      putchar(c);
    }
}
```

The code for the program is easy to interpret. A character variable "c" is declared. Then the input file (designated by the file descriptor fd) is read, character by character. While the character being read is not the end-of-file marker, the character is placed on the standard output device by the primitive **putchar**. When the end-of-file marker is read, the program terminates. *Note that the program introduces the first loop structure, the* **while** *loop, which will be discussed in detail in the next chapter.*

EXERCISES

1. Given the following Pascal code, write the corresponding C code.

   a. write ('Hello out there!');
   b. writeln ('Hello out there!');
   c. a := 10;
      writeln ('Value of a is ',a);
   d. a := 14.639;
      writeln ('Value of a is ',a:2);

2. What is the output of the following C code?

   a. printf ("Hello");
      printf (" out there\n");
   b. printf ("Hello out there\n");
   c. printf ("Hello\n");
      printf (" out there\n");
   d. a =3; b =4; c =5;
      printf ("The sum of %d and %d is %d.",a,b,a+b);

3. Given the following Pascal code, write the corresponding C code.

   ```
   read (firstvalue);
   writeln ('Number just entered was ',firstvalue:5);
   ```

4. What is the result of the following C code?

   ```
   scanf ("%d, %d, %d",&first, &second, &third);
   printf ("%d, %d, %d", first*first, second*second, third*third);
   ```

5. Write a set of C statements that get a number from standard input and print out the square and cube of the number with appropriate messages.
6. Write a set of C statements that get three numbers from standard input and print out their sum and average with appropriate statements.
7. Examine the program in Figure 5.8. Expand this program so that it copies the contents of any file to a file with a new file name. (If you are not familiar with file handling on your system, you may wish to look at Chapter 10 at this time.)
8. Modify the program written in Exercise 7 to merge the contents of the file into a second file at a specified location (as when a specific control-character/marker is encountered in the second file).

CHAPTER 6

Loops in C and Pascal

OVERVIEW OF CONTROL STRUCTURES IN C AND PASCAL

So far we've seen some general features of Pascal and C programs, and we've discussed the types of variables and operators available in each language. We've also taken a brief look at input and output operations in both languages. In the next three chapters, we'll discuss the control structures that are available for use in programs.

Pascal provides a rich and varied set of control structures. It offers several loop structures (the **for** loop, the **while** loop, and the **repeat** . . . **until** loop) and several conditional-branch structures (the **if** . . . **then** . . . **else** structure and the **case** statement). It also provides for an unconditional-branch structure by including the **goto** ⟨label⟩ statement within the language; even though this feature is rarely seen in Pascal programs, it is available for use in situations in which it is absolutely needed.

C also provides a similar set of control structures. The loop structures that are available include the **for** loop, the **while** loop, and the **do** . . . **while** loop, and the conditional structures include the **if** . . . **else** construct as well as the **switch** statement. In addition, C provides for the unconditional-branch with the familiar **goto** ⟨label⟩ statement.

This chapter will focus on a comparison of the loop control structures in Pascal and C, and Chapter 7 will review the conditional- and unconditional-branch constructions that are available.

THE FOR LOOP IN PASCAL AND C

Both C and Pascal share a similar general structure for the **for** loop control structure. In both languages this structure is used to repeat a statement or a block of code (a compound statement) a specified number of times. The number of times that the loop is repeated is controlled by the value of an index variable, and the range of values for the index variable is specified in the header line for the construction.

In Pascal, the general syntax for the **for** statement is as follows:

```
for ⟨index variable⟩ := ⟨start value⟩ to ⟨stop value⟩ do

    ⟨statement⟩;            or            begin
                                              ⟨compound statement⟩
                                          end;
```

In the **for** statement header line, an initial value is assigned to the index variable. This value is incremented with each pass through the loop, and at the top of the loop (before each pass through the loop) this incremented value is tested against the stop value. When the index variable reaches the stop value, a final pass through the loop is completed. The program then progresses to the next statement following the **for** construction.

The **for** statement in C is similar, with the following general syntax:

```
for (firstexpression; secondexpression; thirdexpression)

⟨statement⟩;            or            {
                                          ⟨compound statement⟩;
                                      }
```

In this general syntax, firstexpression is an expression that initializes the index variable. A typical example of firstexpression might be "i = 0", but much more complex assignments are possible. Function calls to assign an initial value to the variable are both possible and common. They are perfectly valid, since firstexpression is terminated by a semicolon, and any legal expression is possible at this location.

Secondexpression is the condition that is tested at the top of each loop. If the tested condition is true, then the statement(s) following the header line is (are) executed, after which the program loops back to the **for** header line and the condition is tested again. If the tested condition is false, the program code in the loop is not repeated and the program progresses to the next statement. A typical example of a secondexpression would be "i <= 100".

Thirdexpression can be thought of as the final statement in the loop code. This expression is often used to alter the value of the index variable. As in so many other situations, C gives the programmer control over the details of program execution. The value of the index variable is not automatically incremented. Thirdexpression can be used to increment or decrement the index variable by a desired amount. A typical example of thirdexpression might be "+ + i".

The **for** statement in C also has other aspects worth mentioning. For instance, some of the expressions in the **for** header line can be omitted, but the semicolons must still be present. If firstexpression is omitted, the index variable must have been initialized previously in the program. If the secondexpression is omitted, there is no condition to test. This situation will produce an infinite loop; without a condition to test, there is no possibility for a negative test to end the loop. The effect of omitting thirdexpression is less serious, since it is largely a convenience that provides a concise way of adding a final line of code to the program loop.

As an aside, I should mention that it is possible to substitute any valid expression for any of the expressions in the **for** *header line. Although it would be poor programming style, any program code—regardless of its relation to the* **for** *loop code—can be inserted into the header line. Firstexpression, secondexpression, and thirdexpression have designated roles, but the determined programmer can use them for any other necessary purpose.*

Figure 6.1 provides a typical example of a **for** loop in Pascal and C. The

FIGURE 6.1 Use of the **for** *statement in Pascal and C.*

Pascal:

```
program counter (input, output);
var
  number : integer;

(* main program *)
begin
    for number := 1 to 100 do
        begin
        writeln ('NUMBER', 'SQUARE');
        writeln (number, number*number);
        end;
end.
```

C:

```
#include <stdio.h>

/* this is the main function */
main ()
{
  for (number = 1; number <= 100; ++ number)
    {
    printf ("number                    square\n");
    printf (" %d                        %d \n", number, number*number);
    }
}
```

short program provided simply prints out the integers between 1 and 100 and their squares, but it illustrates some of the differences between the two constructions.

THE WHILE LOOP IN PASCAL AND C

Whereas the **for** loop is used if the programmer has some knowledge of the number of times that the loop should be repeated, the **while** loop is generally used when the number of repetitions cannot be easily specified in advance. If the programmer wants the loop to be repeated as long as some condition remains true, and when the number of repetitions that will be involved can't be specified, then the **while** loop is probably preferable.

The **while** loop in Pascal has a simple structure, with the following general syntax:

```
while (condition) do
⟨statement⟩;            or        begin
                                      ⟨compound statement⟩;
                                  end;
```

As a rule, the Pascal **while** loop has a condition that is tested at the top of the loop. If the condition is true, then the program code in the loop is repeated. If it is not true, then the program jumps to the next statement following the **while** construct. The conditions that can be tested in Pascal include the relationships between variables, the value of boolean variables, or the results of a call to a boolean function.

The **while** loop in C is very similar. Its general syntax is as follows:

```
while (condition)
⟨statement⟩;            or        {
                                  ⟨compound statement⟩;
                                  }
```

Just as in Pascal, the conditions that can be tested may be relationships between variables, the value of variables, or the results of function calls. Since C does not provide boolean variables per se, the tests of variable values or function calls work a little differently from those in Pascal. In C, any nonzero value is regarded as *true*, and a zero value is considered logically to be *false*. Thus, the results of function calls can be tested as *true* or *false* in this context, based on whether they return a value of zero. Likewise, the value of a variable can be logically tested as true or false, based on whether the value is zero. A typical example of a C program containing a **while** loop is shown in Figure 6.2.

*FIGURE 6.2 The **while** loop in C and Pascal.*

Pascal:

```
program whiledemo (input, output);

var
     number : integer;
     done : boolean;

(* main *)
begin

     (* initialize variables *)
     number := 1;
     done := false;

     (*print integers from 1 to 10 *)
     while (number <= 10) do
          begin
          write ('next integer: ');
          writeln (number);
          number := number + 1;
          end;

     (* test boolean condition *)
     while (not done) do
          begin
          write ('next integer: ');
          writeln (number);
          number := number + 1;
          if (number = 21) then done := true;
          end;

end.
```

C:

```
#include <stdio.h>

/* main function */
main ()
{
     int number;
     int done;

     /* initialize variables */
     number = 1;
     done = 0;

     while (number <= 10)
     {
```

(Figure continued next page)

```
            printf ("next integer: ");
            printf ("%d\n"; number);
            + +number;
            }

        while (! done)
            {
            printf ("next integer: ");
            printf ("%d\n",number);
            + + number;
            if (number >20) done = 1;
            }

        }
```

REPEAT . . . UNTIL IN PASCAL AND DO . . . WHILE IN C

The four loop structures that we have discussed so far (the **for** loop in Pascal and C and the **while** loop in Pascal and C) have one general feature in common: they each have a header line (containing a condition to be tested) and a block of code that follows this header line. The condition is tested *before* the block of code is executed—that is, the condition is tested at the top of the loop.

Both C and Pascal also provide a loop structure in which a condition is tested at the bottom of the loop. In Pascal, this structure is the **repeat . . . until** loop, and in C it is the **do . . . while** loop. Although they are somewhat different, the two structures are sufficiently similar to be discussed together.

The Pascal **repeat . . . until** loop has the following general syntax:

```
repeat

    ⟨statement⟩; or ⟨compound statement⟩;

until ⟨condition⟩;
```

This structure has several important features. First, the block of code which is enclosed within the **repeat** line and the **until** ⟨condition⟩ line will always be executed once. No control over program flow is exerted until the **until** ⟨condition⟩ line is encountered. After the block of code is executed once and the **until** line is encountered, the condition is tested. If the condition is false, then the loop is repeated; if the condition is true, then the loop is not repeated.

A second important feature of this construction is that there is no **begin** and **end** enclosing a compound statement. The **repeat** line and the **until** line replace the **begin** and **end** as the delimiters of the compound statement, and so they are not required here.

A third feature of the **repeat. .until** loop is that the condition being tested usually is initialized to a *false* value. Then the loop is repeated until the condition becomes *true*. In the case of the **for** loop or the **while** loop, this situation is usually reversed; the condition begins with a *true* value and continues until it is *false*.

The **do. . .while** loop in C is similar in structure and function. The general syntax of the **do. . .while** loop is:

```
do
{
    ⟨statement⟩; or ⟨compound statement⟩;
} while ⟨condition⟩;
```

The braces around the statements in the **do** *loop are not formally required. They are common, however, to minimize any possible confusion. Without the braces as delimiters, the terminating* **while** *⟨condition⟩ could be mistaken as the beginning of a* **while** *loop.*

We discussed above three factors of the **repeat. . until** statement in Pascal. Let's compare those three features with the operation of the **do. . .while** statement in C. First of all, the block of code enclosed by the **do** line and the **while** ⟨condition⟩ line is always executed once, just as with the **repeat. . .until** statement. The condition that controls the loop is then tested at the bottom of the loop, after this first pass. The result of the test is somewhat different, though. In the **repeat. . .until** loop, the loop is repeated until the condition becomes true. In the **do. . .while** loop in C, however, the loop is repeated while the condition is true; once it becomes false, then the loop is no longer repeated.

The second feature of the **repeat. . .until** loop that we mentioned was the lack of **begin** and **end** to delimit compound statements. In the **do. . .while** loop, braces should be used to delimit even simple single statements, as mentioned above.

The third feature of the **repeat. . .until** loop was the fact that the controlling condition is usually initialized to a *false* value; the loop then repeats until the value becomes *true*. In the **do. . .while** loop, the condition is usually initialized to a value of *true*, and the loop repeats until the condition is set to a value of *false*.

The condition that is being tested in either of these loops can be either a simple numeric relationship (such as counter >= 10) or a more complex expression. For instance, in the Pascal structure, the condition could be a call to a function that returned a boolean value. In the C structure, any valid expression is permitted, including function calls. As in other loop structures in C, a nonzero value in the condition is regarded as *true* and a value of zero is regarded as *false*.

Figure 6.3 illustrates the **repeat. . .until** structure in Pascal and the **do. . .while** loop in C. *Note that these examples contain* **if. . .then** *statements, which will be discussed further in the next chapter.*

FIGURE 6.3 ***repeat. .until*** *in Pascal and* ***do. .while*** *in C.*

Pascal:

```
program repeatdemo (input, output);

var
    done : boolean;
    number : integer;

(*main program*)
begin
    (*initialize variables*)
    done := false;
    number := 1;

    (* print from 1 to 20*)
    repeat
        writeln ('next integer: ',number);
        number := number + 1;
        if (number >20) then done := true;
    until done;
end.
```

C:

```
#include <stdio.h>

/* main program */
main ()
{
int done, number;

    /* initialize variables */
    done = 0;
    number = 1;

    /* loop and print from 1 to 20 */
    do
    {
        printf ("next integer: %d\n", number);
        ++ number;
        if (number > 20) done = 1;
    }   while (! done);
}
```

SOFTWARE C TOOLS: COUNTING LINES IN A FILE

Figures 6.4, 6.5, and 6.6 illustrate the syntax of the three C loop statements in simple programs. We have also already seen the **while** statement in use; Chapter 5 presented a program that copied files to the standard output, and that program incorporated a simple **while** loop. What other kinds of tools can be constructed using simple loop statements?

Figure 6.7 presents another simple tool. This program counts the number of lines in a file. The program logic is easy to follow and is similar to the tool in the last chapter. Two variables are declared, one a character and one an integer. The file is then read, using the C primitive **getc**, character by character. If the **newline** character is encountered, the integer variable being used as a counter is incremented. When the end-of-file marker is found, the final result is displayed. Notice that this program also introduces the **if** statement, which will be explained in Chapter 7.

*FIGURE 6.4 Sample program illustrating **for** loops in C.*

```
#include <stdio.h>
/*this program demonstrates for loops and arrays*/

/* define a constant */
#define LIMIT 10

/* declare global variables */
int index;
int dataset[11];

/*main: assign values to array, then print out */
main ()
{
     /*assign values and print out immediately */
     for (index =1; index <= 10; + + index)
          {
           dataset[index] = index * index;
           printf("Value of arrayelement %d is %d\n",index,dataset[index]);
          }

     /* print out array again, using for loop and constant */
     for (index=1; index <= LIMIT; + + index)
        printf("Array element: %d              Value: %d\n",index,dataset[index]);
}
```

FIGURE 6.5 Sample program illustrating ***while*** *loops in C.*

```
#include ⟨stdio.h⟩
#define LIMIT 10      /* define constant LIMIT */

/*declare global variables*/
int index;
int dataset[11];

/*main: assign values to array with while loop and print out */
main()
{
     index = 1;     /*initialize index */
     while (index <= LIMIT)
     {
          dataset[index] = index * index;
          printf ("Arrayelement: %d      Value: %d\n",index,dataset[index]);
          ++index;
     }
}
```

FIGURE 6.6 Sample program illustrating use of ***do. .while*** *loops in C.*

```
#include ⟨stdio.h⟩
/*this demonstrates do-while loops*/

#define LIMIT 10      /*define constant LIMIT */

/* declare global variables */
int index;
int dataset[11];

/*main:     assign values to array elements and print out */
main()
{
  index = 1;     /*initialize index */

     /*use do while loop to assign values and print out*/
     do
       { dataset[index] = index * index;
         printf ("Arrayelement: %d      Value: %d\n",index, dataset[index]);
         ++index;
       }
       while (index <= LIMIT);     /*end do-while loop*/
}
```

FIGURE 6.7 This program illustrates the use of loops and conditional statements in C. (Note: The file "list.c" is opened in this program using the special file specifier demanded by a CP/M compiler. The file specifier on your system may differ. Consult your system manual for details of the use of the function ***getc***.*)*

```
#include <stdio.h>
#define EOF -1

int numline;
char c;

/* main function opens a file name "list.c",         */
/* reads it line by line, and increments a            */
/* counter whenever a newline marker is found.   */

main ()
{
     /* initialize value of counter */
     numline = 0;

     /* open file and read characters until EOF */
     while ((c = getc ("O/A: list.c ")) != EOF)
          {
               /* if newline is encountered, increment counter . . . */
               if ( c = = '\n' )
                    + +numline;
          };

     /* display results */
     printf ("%d\n", numline);

}
```

EXERCISES

1. Given the following Pascal code, write the corresponding C code.

a.
```
for counter := 1 to 100 do
     writeln (counter);
```

b.
```
for counter := 1 to 100 do
  begin
     write ('Hello ');
     writeln (' out there!');
  end;
```

c.
```
a := 1;
for counter := 1 to 100 do
   begin
   writeln ('a = ',a,'; squared = ',a*a);
   a := a +1;
   end;
```

2. Given the following Pascal code, write the corresponding C code.

a.
```
counter := 1;
while (counter < 100) do
   begin
   writeln (counter);
   counter := counter +1;
   end;
```

b.
```
counter := 1;
repeat
   writeln (counter);
   counter := counter +1;
until counter =100;
```

c.
```
done := false;
while (not done) do
   begin
   a := a *a;
   b := b *b;
   . . .⟨more code⟩
   end;
```

3. What is the output of the following C code?

a.
```
for (c =1; c < 100; ++c)
   { printf ("%d",c);
   }
```

b.
```
for (c=1; c<100; ++a)
   { printf("%d, %d\n",a,c);
   }
```

c.
```
a = 4;
while (a < 100)
   { printf ("%d\n",a);
     a *= a;
   }
```

4. Write the C code for loops that will

a. print a table of squares for integers from 1 to 100
b. print all odd integers between 1 and 100
c. print the Fibonacci series for values less than 100

The Fibonacci series consists of the numbers 1,2,3,5,8,13, . . . , where each number is the sum of the two previous numbers.

5. Write a C program that inputs a series of Fahrenheit temperatures from the keyboard and then prints out the corresponding Celsius values. When the user enters some appropriate flag value (such as 9999), the program should end. *The conversion formula is:* $C = (F - 32) * (5/9)$.

6. Examine the demonstration program in Figure 6.7. Modify the line-counter program so that it prints out on the standard output the contents of any file, with an appropriate line number preceding each line.

7. Examine the demonstration line-counter program in Figure 6.7. How would the program need to be modified to count characters? To count words? Write a program that reads a file and prints out the total number of characters and the total number of words in the file.

CHAPTER 7

Conditional Statements and Branching

OVERVIEW OF CONDITIONAL STATEMENTS IN C AND PASCAL

This chapter will survey the conditional structures that are available in C and Pascal. Pascal provides the **if. .then. .else** statement (which is common in most algorithmic languages), and it also provides the **case** statement for choosing among possible program options. C also has the familiar **if. .else** statement and the **switch** statement, which is analogous to the Pascal **case** statement.

Since branching within a program is often the result of a conditional statement, it will also be considered here. Both languages permit **conditional branching** (as the result of a conditional statement) and **unconditional branching** (by which program flow is unconditionally directed elsewhere in a program). Unconditional branching is implemented through the familiar **goto** statement. Both C and Pascal use the **goto** statement in association with a label, and the use is very similar in both languages.

THE IF . . . STATEMENT IN C AND PASCAL

Both languages have a basic conditional statement, and that statement is the **if. .then. .else** in Pascal and the analogous **if. .else** in C. Although the details of their use differ slightly, these two statements have a similar function and effect.

The Pascal **if. .then. .else** statement has the following general syntax:

```
if ⟨condition⟩
    then
    ⟨statement⟩          or        begin
                                   ⟨compound statement⟩;
                                   end

    else
    ⟨statement⟩;         or        begin
                                   ⟨compound statement⟩;
                                   end;
```

The **else** part of the statement is optional. If there is no **else** in the statement, then there would generally be a semicolon at the end of the **if** construct to separate it from following statements in the program.

The **if. .then. .else** statement can also be expanded significantly. Since the **if. .then. .else** statement is itself a valid statement, further **if. .then. .else** statements can be embedded into it. Thus, the following construct is perfectly valid:

```
if (condition 1)
  then
    ⟨statement 1⟩

  else
    if (condition 2)
      then
        ⟨statement 2⟩
      else
        ⟨statement 3⟩;
```

A similar construct exists in C: the **if. .else** statement. The general syntax of the **if. .else** statement in C follows:

```
if ⟨condition⟩

  ⟨statement 1⟩; or {⟨compound statement⟩;}
      else
      ⟨statement 2⟩; or {⟨compound statement⟩;}
```

The program flow through this construct follows the same rules as for the Pascal **if. .then. .else.** The condition is tested; if it is true, then the statement (or compound statement) following the **if** is executed. If it is false, then the statement (or compound statement) following the **else** is executed.

There are, however, some differences between the two conditional statements. The condition that is tested in the C statement is any valid expression. It could be a simple test of numeric relationships (such as "if (number < = 10) . . .") or a more complex expression or a function call. Remember that whenever a condition is tested in C and an expression is being evaluated as the test, the value of the expression is all that's important. If the expression evaluates to a nonzero value, then it is logically regarded as *true*. If the expression evaluates to zero, then it is logically regarded as *false*.

Another significant difference is seen in the use of semicolons. In the Pascal **if. .then. .else** statement, a semicolon is never used before an **else** statement. In C, however, the semicolon is a statement terminator and is required as an essential element of each statement. A statement that follows **if . . .** is terminated by a semicolon, even if such a statement is placed before an **else. . . .** Therefore, a semicolon is often seen before the **else** part in a C conditional statement. For an example of the different syntax in Pascal and C, see Figure 7.1. Figure 7.2 provides typical examples of the use of the **if . . .** statements in Pascal and C.

*FIGURE 7.1 The use of semicolons in **if**. . . statements.*

	RIGHT	WRONG
Pascal:	if (cond) then writeln ('HI!') else . . .	if (cond) then writeln ('HI!'); else . . .
C:	if (cond) printf ("HI!\n"); else . . .	if (cond) printf("HI!\n") else . . .

*FIGURE 7.2 The **if**. .statements in Pascal and C.*

Pascal:

```
program ifdemo (input, output);
var
   value : integer;
   done : boolean;

(* main program *)
begin
   (* initialize variables *)
   value := 1;
   done := false;
```

```
(* loop until square of value exceeds 1000*)
while (not done) do
     begin
     write ('Enter a value: ');
     readln (value);
     writeln ('Your value squared is: ',value * value);
     if (value * value > 1000)
          then
               begin
                    writeln ('The square is greater than 1000.');
                    done := true
               end
          else
               writeln ('The square is <= 1000.');
     end;
end.
```

C:

```
#include <stdio.h>
/* main program */
main()
  {
     int value, done;

     /* initialize variables */
          value = 1;
          done = 0;

     /*loop until square of value exceeds 1000*/
          while (! done)
               {
               printf ("Enter a value: ");
               scanf ("%d\n", &value);
               printf ("Your value squared is: %d\n ",value*value);
               if (value* value > 1000)
                    {
                    printf("The square is greater than 1000.\n");
                    done = 1;
                    }
                    else
                         {
                         printf("The square is <= 1000.\n");
                         }
               }
  }
```

THE PASCAL CASE STATEMENT AND THE C SWITCH STATEMENT

Sometimes a program may contain a point at which one of several options should be exercised. This programming situation can be handled by using a multiple **if . . .** statement, in which nested **if**s can test a series of conditions, and when the first condition is found that evaluates as *true*, then the corresponding block of code can be executed.

Often, however, it is much easier to solve this situation with a statement specifically designed for handling multiple options. In Pascal, the answer is the **case** statement. The general syntax for the **case** statement follows:

```
case ⟨selector⟩ of

    ⟨value 1⟩:    ⟨statement 1⟩;
    ⟨value 2⟩:    ⟨statement 2⟩;
    . . .
    ⟨value n⟩:    ⟨statement n⟩;
    end;
```

The **case** statement is controlled by the value of a selector, which is a scalar variable. Depending upon the value of the selector variable, one of several possible blocks of code may be executed. (For instance, if the selector has a value equal to value 1, then statement 1 will be executed.) Following execution of the appropriate block of code, program flow passes on to the next statement after the **end**, which closes the **case** statement.

Several points are important about the **case** statement in Pascal. First, the selector must be a scalar variable. Second, all possible values for the selector must be defined in the list of case options; if the selector has a value for which there is no matching case option, then a run-time error will occur. Third, if no action is to be taken when the selector has certain values, those values must still be listed, followed by an empty statement list and a semicolon.

It should also be noted that the **case** statement ends with the word **end,** but there is no matching **begin;** this is the only such case in Pascal. In addition, although the diagram above shows simple statements to be executed in each case option, a compound statement is equally possible. For the sake of brevity, only the simple statement has been indicated.

C has a statement analogous to the Pascal **case** statement: the **switch** statement. The general syntax of the **switch** statement is as follows:

```
switch (⟨expression⟩)
    {
    case ⟨value 1⟩: ⟨statement 1⟩;
    case ⟨value 2⟩: ⟨statement 2⟩;
    case ⟨value 3⟩: ⟨statement 3⟩;
     . . .
```

```
case ⟨value n⟩:  ⟨statement n⟩;
default:         ⟨default statement⟩;
}
```

The **switch** statement may superficially resemble the **case** statement, but there are some major differences in the way they work. First, the expression in the **switch** statement is evaluated, with a result that must be of type int. Then that value is compared with the case labels (which must be constants or constant expressions of type int) that follow the **switch.**

When a match is found, the statement (or compound statement) corresponding to that case label is executed. Then something very different from the Pascal **case** statement occurs: the case labels in the **switch** statement are really only labels, and program execution will continue with the next executable statement *within* the **switch** statement. For example, if the ⟨expression⟩ matched ⟨value 1⟩, then ⟨statement 1⟩ would be executed, followed by ⟨statement 2⟩, ⟨statement 3⟩, and so on.

In some cases, this construct may be desirable. *For instance, you may want the same code to be executed for several case label matches. In that case, you could list a sequence of case labels, followed by the code to be executed. Then when any match in that list occurred, the program would "fall through" to the common code to be executed.* On the other hand, you would usually want the same sort of control that the Pascal **case** statement gives you; that is, once the code for a given case label is executed, you would want to proceed to the next executable program statement *after* the **switch** statement.

This alternate flow can be accomplished with the **break** statement in C, which causes the program to exit the **switch** statement and proceed to the next program statement. If you end the block of code for each case with a **break** statement, then the program will execute that block of code and then exit the **switch** statement. The effect will be very similar to that seen in the Pascal **case.**

What happens if there is no match between the expression value and any of the case labels? Note that the **switch** statement contains a default case label to handle this situation. If there is no match, then the block of code following the default case label is executed. The default case label is optional; if there is no default case label and there is no match between expression and case label, then no case options are executed and program flow passes on to the next executable statement.

Figure 7.3 illustrates the use of the Pascal **case** statement and the C **switch** statement.

BRANCHING IN PASCAL AND C WITH GOTO AND BREAK

Both Pascal and C provide for branching under the control of the familiar **goto** statement. The syntax in both Pascal and C is similar, with the **goto** state-

*FIGURE 7.3 The **case** statement in Pascal and **switch** in C.*

Pascal:

```
program casedemo (input,output);
var
    number : integer;

(*main program*)
begin
    write ('Enter number between 1 and 5: ');
    readln (number);

    if (number<1) or (number>5)
      then
          writeln ('Number out of range')
      else
          case number of
                1 : writeln ('Your number is one.');
                2 : writeln ('Your number is two.');
                3 : writeln ('Your number is three.');
                4 : writeln ('Your number is four.');
                5 : begin
                    writeln ('Your number is five.');
                    writeln ('This is largest number.');
                    end;
          end; (*case*)
end.
```

C:

```
#include <stdio.h>

/* main function */
 main ()
{
int number;

printf("Enter a number between 1 and 5: ");
scanf ("%d\n", &number);

if (number < 1) || (number > 5)
     {
     printf ("Number out of range\r");
     }
     else
          switch (number)
               {case 1: printf ("Your number is one.\r");
                        break;
                case 2: printf ("Your number is two.\r");
                        break;
```

FIGURE 7.3 (Continued)

```
                    case 3: printf("Your number is three.\n");
                            break;
                    case 4: printf("Your number is four.\n");
                            break;
                    case 5: printf("Your number is five.\n");
                            printf("This is largest number.\n");
                            break;
                    default: /* using this optional case label      */
                            /* to handle non-match makes it       */
                            /* unnecessary to nest SWITCH in */
                            /* the IF. . statement.                 */
                            printf("Number is out of range.\n");
                            break;
               }
    }
```

ment being associated with a label. In the Pascal **goto** statement, the general syntax is as follows:

```
label
    ⟨labelname 1⟩, ⟨labelname 2⟩, . . .
        =
        =
        goto ⟨labelname 1⟩;
        =
        =
⟨labelname 1⟩: ⟨statements⟩;
```

The labels to be used must be declared at the top of the main program or a procedure or a function, preceding the type declarations and var declarations. Labelnames must be integers. In the body of the program code, a **goto** followed by the labelname will direct program flow unconditionally to the program statement preceded by that labelname.

A **goto** statement in C is also used in association with a label, and it directs program flow unconditionally to the statement associated with the label. The general syntax is identical. The word **goto** is followed by a labelname, which can be any valid C identifier name. When the line is encountered, program flow is directed to the statement line preceded by the labelname and a colon.

C also provides another statement for redirecting program flow. This is the **break** statement, just introduced in our discussion of the **switch** statement. In the **switch** statement, the **break** can be used to force program execution out of the **switch** options on to the next executable statement after the **switch**. The **break** statement can also be used inside **for** loops, **while** loops, and **do** loops. When the **break** statement is encountered, the program immediately exits from the current loop.

The **break** statement will, therefore, handle most of the situations for which the **goto** might be needed in Pascal. The **goto** statement in C has only limited usefulness. In most cases it is only rarely used. One of the few programming situations in which it might be effective is in exiting from deeply nested loops; whereas a series of **break** statements could be used to sequentially exit from each loop, a simple **goto** that leaves the entire structure would probably be the simplest solution.

Figure 7.4 illustrates the use of **goto** statements in C and Pascal, and Figure 7.5 demonstrates the use of the **break** statement in C.

FIGURE 7.4 Use of ***goto*** *in Pascal and C.*

Pascal:

```
program gotodemo (input, output);
label
    10;
var
    number1, number2 : integer;

begin

    for number1 := 1 to 1000 do
        begin
            for number2 := 1 to 1000 do
                begin
                    writeln (number1, number2);
                    if (number1*number1 > 500)
                        then goto 10
                end;
        end;

10: writeln ('end of loop');

end.
```

C:

```
#include <stdio.h>

main ()
{
    int number1, number2;
```

FIGURE 7.4 (Continued)

```
      for (number1 = 1; number1 = 1000; + + number1)
          {
              for (number2=1; number2=1000;+ +number2)
                  {
                  printf (" %d, %d\n", number1, number2);
                  if (number1*number1 > 500)
                     goto loopout;
                  }
          }
      loopout: printf("end of loop\n");
  }
```

FIGURE 7.5 Use of **break** *in C.*

C:

```
  #include <stdio.h>

  main()
  {
     int number;

     /* loop will continue until square exceeds 500 */
     /* then BREAK will force exit from loop.        */

               for (number=1; number =1000; + + number)
               {
                    printf("%d,%d\n",number, number*number);
                    if (number*number > 500)
                         break;
               }
  }
```

SOFTWARE C TOOLS: FILTER PROGRAM

Figures 7.6 and 7.7 provide examples of the **if. . else** statement and the **switch** statement in simple C programs. Can we produce a more useful tool by using the constructs that have been presented so far?

Figure 7.8 presents an example of a useful class of tools called **filters.** Filters are programs that take input and process selected elements of the in-

FIGURE 7.6 Sample program illustrating ***if*** *. .***else***. . . statement in C.*

```
#include <stdio.h>
/* this demonstrates if. . .else statements */

#define LIMIT 10

/* declare global variables */
int index;
int dataset[11];

/* main: assign array values, then scan fo- values > 50*/
main()
{
     /* assign array values */
     for (index = 1; index <= LIMIT; + + index)
          dataset[index] = index * index;

     /* look at values; print out if <=50 o- >50 */
     for (index = 1; index <= LIMIT; + -index)
       {
          if (dataset[index] > 50)
                    printf ("Arrayelement %d has value > 50",index);
             else
                    printf ("Arrayelement %d has value <= 50",index);
          printf("\n");
       }
}
```

FIGURE 7.7 Sample program illustrating use of ***switch*** *statement in C.*

```
#include <stdio.h>
/*this demonstrates use of switch statement */

#define LIMIT 10             /*this defines constant LIMIT*/

/* declare global variables */
int index;
int dataset[11];

/* main: assign array values, then scan array with switch */
main()
{
     /* assign array values */
     for (index = 1; index <= LIMIT; + +index)
          dataset[index] = index * index;
```

FIGURE 7.7 (Continued)

```
    /*scan array with switch statement */
    for (index = 1; index <= LIMIT; ++index)
        switch (index)
        { case 1: printf("This is array element 1\n");
                  break;
          case 2: printf("This is array element 2\n");
                  break;
          case 3: printf ("This is array element 3\n");
                  break;
          default: printf("This is array element 4 or greater\n");
                  break;
        }
}
```

FIGURE 7.8 This program demonstrates the use of conditional statements and simple I/O in C.

```
#include <stdio.h>
    /* main function gets a character from the keyboard, */
    /* tests to see if it is upper or lower case,         */
    /* and converts it to upper case if it is lower.      */

    main()
    {
      char g;

            /*get a character . . . */
            scanf ("%c", &g);

            /*convert lower case letter to upper case . . . */
            if ( g >= 'a' && g <= 'z')

                g = g + 'A' - 'a';

            /* output the result . . . */
            printf (" %c\n", g);
    }
```

put into a predetermined output pattern. This particular filter takes a character as input; if it is uppercase, the character is output, but if it is lowercase, it is converted to uppercase and then output.

Basically, a character is assigned a value. Then the **if** statement checks whether it is in the range of ASCII values corresponding to lowercase letters. If the character is not lowercase, it is printed. If it is lowercase, then it is assigned a new value, which is the ASCII code of the corresponding uppercase letter; then the new character is output.

If the contents of a string were to be converted from lowercase to uppercase, then this code would need to be used repeatedly. It is therefore a logical choice to be defined as a function that can be called repetitively. The use of functions in C is the topic of the next chapter, and the corresponding code is provided at the end of that chapter.

EXERCISES

1. Given the following Pascal code, write the corresponding C code:

a.
```
if (a < 10)
   then b := a + c;
```

b.
```
if (a < 10)
   then b := a + c
   else b := a * a;
```

c.
```
if (a < 10)
   then
       begin
       b := a + c;
       writeln (b);
       end
   else
       begin
       b := a * a;
       writeln (b);
       end;
```

d.
```
if (a < 10)
   then
       b := a + c
   else
   if (a <20)
       then b:= a * a;
```

2. Given the following Pascal code, write the corresponding C code.

a.
```
read (a);
case a of
```

```
1 : writeln ('a = 1');
2 : writeln ('a = 2');
3 : writeln ('a = 3');
end;
```

b.
```
read (b);
if ( (b > 3) or (b < 0 ))
  then writeln ('error - b out of range')
  else
    begin
    writeln ('b in acceptable range');
    case b of
      1 : writeln ('b = 1');
      2 : writeln ('b = 2');
      3 : writeln ('b = 3);
      end;
    end;
```

3. Write a C program that inputs an integer value between 1 and 10. Print out a message indicating whether the integer is even or odd.
4. Write a C program that inputs ten integer values between 1 and 10. Print the ten values out in sorted order.
5. Write a C program that inputs a character. Print a message indicating whether the character is a letter, number, or punctuation mark.
6. Examine the demonstration program, "lower-to-upper", in Figure 7.8. That program converts all lowercase characters to uppercase before output. Modify the program so that it converts the uppercase letters to lowercase (that is, so that all output is lowercase).
7. Write a program that gets a line of input from standard input and prints out the entire line in uppercase, regardless of the case of the input characters.
8. Write a program that gets a line of input from standard input and prints out the entire line in lowercase, regardless of the case of the input characters.
9. Write a filter that gets a line of input from standard input. If the line contains an integer (0. .9), have the correct text (zero . . . nine) inserted for the integer.

CHAPTER 8

Functions and Parameter Passing in Pascal and C

OVERVIEW OF SUBPROGRAMS IN PASCAL AND C

C and Pascal share a common view on program development. Both languages encourage the development of programs in a specific way—breaking down a programming problem into its component subtasks and writing a block of code to handle each of those subtasks. A program, therefore, is a collection of component subprograms, with some main program code included to initiate the program and control the execution of component subprograms. In Pascal, there are two kinds of subprograms: **procedures** and **functions**. In C, **functions** are the only available type of subprogram.

Pascal procedures and functions are similar. A procedure can be called, passed parameters, and may change the value of the passed parameters, local variables, or global variables. Functions perform the same sort of operations, but they also return a value for the function name. *In many ways, procedures can be conceptually considered as subsets of functions: a procedure can do everything a function does except return a value for its name.*

Functions in C are very similar to Pascal functions. They can be called, passed input parameter values, and may return values from the function. The precise way in which these are accomplished, however, is different from Pascal.

When you consider the overall structure of C and Pascal programs, one basic structural difference quickly becomes obvious. Pascal programs consist of a collection of procedures and functions; in addition, they contain a block of code at the end of the program, delimited by **begin** . . . **end.** That is the main program. Program execution begins with this main program code, and functions and procedures are to have been defined above it.

The equivalent code in a C program is handled differently. In a C program, there must always be one function named **main,** and program execution begins with this function. Although the location of this main function is arbitrary, by convention it is usually listed as the first function in the program. Thus, C and Pascal programs have a different overall organization: a Pascal program contains a series of procedure and function definitions, followed by the main program code; and a C program consists of a series of function definitions, one of which must be named **main**.

FUNCTION DEFINITIONS IN PASCAL AND C

Pascal procedures and functions are defined in similar ways. Since there is no equivalent structure in C for the Pascal procedure, we will concentrate on Pascal function definitions and the related C program structures. A Pascal function is defined in the following way:

```
⟨function name⟩ (parameter1: ⟨type⟩; . . . ):⟨type returned⟩;
    ⟨constant declarations⟩
    ⟨type definitions⟩
    ⟨variable declarations⟩
      begin
        ⟨function code⟩;
      end;
```

The name of the function is followed by a list of input parameters. This is a list of variables that will be assigned values when the function is called. *These are often called* **formal parameters***; the values that will be passed into these formal parameters from the calling statements are often called the* **actual parameters**. Each variable on the formal parameter list must be typed in the header line.

The input parameter list is followed by a declaration of the type of the value that will be assigned to the function name. This is followed by optional const, type, and var declaration sections. Types or variables declared in these sections will be local in scope.

After these declarations come the actual function code, enclosed by **begin . . . end;**. In the function code, a statement must be included that will assign a value to the function name; that is, there must be a statement line such as:

```
⟨function name⟩ := . . . . ⟨some value assigned⟩;
```

When the function is exited, that value will be returned for the function name.

Function definitions in C are similar in structure. The general format of a C function definition is as follows:

FIGURE 8.1 Program "errormessage" defines the function named "panic" and calls it from the main function.

```
#include ⟨stdio.h⟩
panic()
{
   printf("this is an error message\n")
   return;
}

main()
{
panic();
}
```

```
⟨type returned⟩ ⟨function name⟩ (parm1  parm2, . . . )
⟨types of the parameter list variables⟩;
{
        ⟨types of local variables⟩;
        ⟨function code⟩;
}
```

Several syntax differences are immediately apparent. First, the type of the value that will be returned from the function is specified at the beginning, rather than the end, of the header line. Second, the types of the variables on the formal parameter list are not specified within the parentheses on the header line; rather, they are specified in their own variable-type declaration section following the parameter list. Third, the local variables are typed after the opening braces; if you have been thinking of the opening braces as equivalent to the Pascal **begin**, then certainly this type declaration section is in a different location from its counterpart in a Pascal program.

A short C program containing a function definition and call is seen in Figure 8.1.

DIFFERENCES BETWEEN PASCAL AND C FUNCTIONS

So far we have discussed some minor differences in the syntax of function definitions in C and Pascal, but there are several more important differences. These major differences are the importance of the sequence of function definitions, the type of the value returned by the function, and the means by which the return value is determined.

In Pascal, the sequence of function (and procedure) definitions is very important. When a function (or procedure) is called in the program, it must have been defined previously in the program code. An attempt to reference a subprogram that has not been previously defined will generally result in a compile-time error.

Actually, the Pascal subprogram need not have been completely defined. It must, however, have been at least previously mentioned in a **forward** *statement. This Pascal statement specifies the subprogram name and parameter list and indicates that the subprogram itself will be defined later in the program.*

The sequence of C function definitions, on the other hand, is governed by different rules. By convention, the **main** function is generally placed first, but the other definitions may be placed in any convenient order. As long as the functions return values of type **int**, then the order is largely irrelevant. *If the functions return values other than type* **int**, *then the sequence is more constrained. See the next section, "Declaring Functions in C."* In fact, C function definitions may even be grouped in different files, which can be linked when the program is compiled.

Another difference between C and Pascal concerns the type of the value that is returned by the function defined. Pascal functions can return a value of any standard type for the function name, and the type returned must be listed on the header line following the parameter list and preceded by a colon. In C, however, although the function may return any valid type, a default type is built into the language. If no other type is specified, then the function is assumed to return a value of type **int**. Put another way, if the value to be returned is of type **int** (which is very often the case), then no return type needs to be specified on the function header line. Only if a type other than **int** is to be returned as the function value does it need to be specified on the header line.

The third major difference that we need to discuss is the means by which the return value is determined. In Pascal, the return value is calculated by a statement line that assigns a value to the function name. Thus, every Pascal function needs to contain a statement line that looks like this:

⟨function name⟩ := . . . (value assigned)

On the other hand, a C function does not contain a line that assigns a value to the function name. Instead, a C function may contain one or more **return** statements. The syntax of a **return** statement is as follows:

```
return (expression);
```

Whenever a **return** statement is encountered in the function code, the expression is evaluated. After the expression is evaluated, the function is exited, and that value is returned as the value of the function. More than one **return** statement may be included within a single function's code, since they can be embedded within **if** . . . statements or **switch** statements, with one **return** encountered if one condition were true and another **return** if another condition were true.

Although a **return** statement is not formally required within a C function, it is much better style to include one in each function definition. If no **return** statement has been encountered in a function by the time the closing brace is encountered, then control returns to the calling program statement, but the value for the function is random and meaningless.

DECLARING FUNCTIONS IN C

What happens if a C function is called and has not been previously defined in the file? It depends on two things: whether the function is defined later in the same file or in another source file altogether. If the function definition is found later in the same file, and if it returns a value of type **int**, then no further programming effort is required. If, on the other hand, the function returns another type, or if it is found in another file, then the function must be "declared" before it is called. *This declaration is somewhat analogous to the use of* **forward** *statements in Pascal.*

For instance, consider the following schematic code:

```
#include ⟨stdio.h⟩

main()
    { char name1();
      char a;
      int b;
      b = name2;
      a = name1;
    }

int name2
    { function name2 code }

char name1
    { function name1 code }
```

The function "name2" can be accessed without previously declaring its type, since it returns type **int**. Function "name 1," however, returns type **char** and must therefore be declared prior to its call. The syntax of the declaration statement is straightforward:

```
⟨type⟩ ⟨function name⟩ ();
```

PARAMETER PASSING IN PASCAL AND C

In Pascal, functions can be called by a statement naming the function and providing a list of input values for the formal parameter list. For instance, consider the following schematic code:

```
program showfunction (input, output);
var
    c: integer;
    d,e : real;

function demo (a:integer; b: real) : real;
    begin
      a := a*a;
      b :=b*b;
      demo :=a*b;
    end;

(* main *)
    begin
    c := 3;
    d := 4;
    e := demo (c,d);
    writeln (c,d,e);
    end.
```

When the main program code executes, values are assigned to c and d. Then the function is called by being named, and it is passed the values of c and d. (The variables c and d are often called "actual parameters," to distinguish them from the "formal parameters" which follow the function name on the function header line.) In the function header line, those input values are assigned to the formal parameters a and b. In the function code, the values of a and b are altered, and then the function return value is determined. This return value is assigned to variable e in the main program.

In this example, the values of c and d in the main program remain unaffected by the statements in the function code. When the function is called, the values of c and d were copied over into a and b and used locally within the function, but these copies had no effect on the values of c and d. This type of parameter passing is known as **call by value**; the values of the actual parameters are passed, and what happens to those formal parameters has no effect on the value of the original actual parameters.

Pascal does provide a mechanism by which the value of the original actual parameters can be changed by the function code. Consider the effect of the following change to the function header line:

```
function demo (var a: integer; var b :real) : real;
```

Now, when the function is called, the values of c and d will be assigned to the formal parameters a and b. In the function code, the values of a and b will be changed, and the return value for the function will be determined. When control returns to the main program, however, the values of the actual parameters (variables c and d) will have been changed by the statements in the function body. The variables c and d will have been assigned the new values of variables a and b.

Why is this true? The addition of the word *var* before the variable names in the function formal parameter list causes a different relationship to exist between the actual parameters and the formal parameters. Now the function is being **called by reference**. When the function is called, the values of the actual parameters are not copied into the formal parameters for use in the function. Instead, the addresses of the actual parameters are passed to the function. In a very real sense, the actual parameters are temporarily renamed; the memory locations in which those values are stored are now addressed by the formal parameters in the function. Whenever a change occurs to those formal parameters, the actual parameters are also changed.

What happens in a C function call? C has no exact equivalent to this Pascal **var** declaration. Under normal situations, any call to a function in C is **call by value**. That is, parameter passing in C most closely resembles the Pascal situation in which there are no **var** declarations within the formal parameter list.

For example, consider the following C function code:

```
#include <stdio.h>
int c;
float d,e;

float function1 (a,b)
  int a;
  float b;
{
  a = a*a;
  b = b*b;
  return (a*b);
}

main ()
{
        c = 3;
        d = 4;
        e = function1 (c,d);
        printf("%d,%d,%d",c,d,e);
}
```

In this example, the main function executes and assigns values to the variables c and d. Then the function is called and passed the values of the actual parameters c and d. The function is **called by value**; that is, the formal parameters a and b are assigned the values of the actual parameters, but those values are only copies of the actual parameter values, used temporarily within the function. What happens to those values has no effect on the actual parameters c and d.

Can C functions be written in such a way that the actual parameters can be changed by alterations in the values of the formal parameters? They can, but this will involve the use of pointers. If you wish to effectively call the function by reference, then you must pass not the *value* of the actual parame-

FIGURE 8.2 Sample program illustrating function definitions and function calls in C.

```
#include <stdio.h>
/* demonstrates basic function definitions */

/*function to total input values passed to it*/
int gettotal     (first, second, third)
int first, second, third;     /*declare parameter types*/

{ int total;     /*declare local variable types*/

      total = first + second + third;

      /*return value for function name*/
      return(total);
}

/*main: get three values and find total */
main()
{ int a,b,c,sum;     /*declare local var types*/

      a = 3; b = 5; c = 6;     /*initialize values*/

      sum = gettotal(a,b,c);

      printf("The total is %d\n",sum);
}
```

ters but rather the *address* of the actual parameters. To pass the address of the actual parameters, you must pass a pointer to that memory location. This procedure will be covered in the next chapter, which deals with pointers in some detail.

A typical example of a C program containing a function definition with parameters and call is seen in Figure 8.2.

ARGUMENTS FOR THE main FUNCTION: ARGC AND ARGV

The **main** function represents a special problem for the C programmer. When the compiled program is executed, it would be useful to supply initial values for some variables at run-time. C permits the user to supply these values (called **command-line arguments**) by passing them to two special variables, **argc** and **argv**.

Argc and **argv** are special C variables. **Argc** will store the number of command-line arguments, and **argv** is a pointer to an array of strings that will store the actual argument values.

To understand this, you must understand how C programs are executed. In most environments, a C program will be executed by naming it, along with any optional arguments, on a command line. For instance, if the system prompt is % and the name of the executable program file is "demo1," then the command line

```
% demo1 ⟨newline⟩
```

would execute the program. Similarly, if the program name were "sort" and you wanted your program to sort four names (e.g., "Tom," "Kelly," "Nancy," and "John"), then the command line might be:

```
% sort Tom Kelly Nancy John ⟨newline⟩
```

In the first example, the function **main** is called with no arguments. The actual header line for the function would look like this:

```
main ()
```

and the conventional operations that we have already discussed would occur.

In the second example, however, the situation is somewhat different. The command line contains the program name ("sort") and four arguments. **Argc** (which stores the **count** of the number of command-line arguments) would equal five—the program name plus four actual parameters. **Argv** (a pointer called the argument **vector**) would be a pointer to an array consisting of five strings. Argv[0] equals the program name, argv[1] equals the name "Tom," argv[2] equals the name "Kelly," etc. The header line for the **main** function would be:

```
main (argc, argv)
int argc;
char *argv[];
{ ⟨main function code . . . ⟩}
```

Within the main function code, the values on the original command line can now be accessed and used as any other variables.

RECURSION AND NESTED FUNCTION DEFINITIONS

Two related topics will complete our survey of functions in Pascal and C: the use of **recursion** and **nested function definitions**.

Recursion is the process in which a function is called from within itself. One of Pascal's most powerful features, it is also available in C. The use of recursion is generally memory intensive. When the function is called from within itself, the current values within the function are stored on a stack, and each successive call places successive layers of values on the stack. When the function is exited, these layers of values are retrieved in reverse order from the stack. Recursion provides an elegant solution for some programming problems, such as the coding of tree traversals or quicksort algorithms. In such cases, the clarity of the code may be more important than the memory overhead associated with the use of recursion.

Although both languages support the use of recursion (in which the function may be thought to be nested several times within itself), only Pascal supports the true definition of functions within functions. In Pascal, it is possible to define a function, and within that function to define other functions that are local in scope to the original function. C does not support the definition of nested functions. Although this may be occasionally inconvenient, it reflects the simple overall structure of the language.

SOFTWARE C TOOLS: FILTER PROGRAM WITH FUNCTIONS

In the last chapter, we introduced how C loop statements and conditional statements could be used to construct a small filter program. That program took a character, determined if it were lowercase, and converted it to uppercase if necessary. In general, that program showed how to design a filter to take any character input and display the output in uppercase characters.

Figure 8.3 presents a similar program. This filter contains several elements of the program as functions that are called at appropriate points. The program also processes entire lines, rather than single characters.

FIGURE 8.3 Use of C functions to input a line of characters and print out the line in uppercase letters.

```
#include <stdio.h>
#define MAXLEN 255

/* Main function gets line of characters and calls */
/* function ltou to process line. Process will end  */
/*when an empty string is entered at keyboard.   */
main ()
    {
    int maxchar, len;
    char inputline [MAXLEN], line [MAXLEN];
    maxchar = 0;

    while ((len = getline (inputline, MAXLEN)) > 0)
        if (( maxchar = ltou (line) = 255)
            len = 0;

    }
```

```
/* function ltou checks array of characters, */
/* outputs character if uppercase,           */
/* converts to uppercase if lowercase.       */
ltou (upline)
char upline [];
    {
    int index;

    index = 0;

    /* while the end-of-string character is not found, */
    /* keep checking each character of array . . .     */
    while (upline [index] != '\0')
            {
              /*if char is lowercase. . . */
              if (upline[index] >= 'a' && upline[index] <= 'z')

                  /* then convert to uppercase and output . . .*/
                  printf ("%c", upline[index] + 'A' - 'a')

                  /* else output the character . */
                  else printf ("%c", upline[index]);

              /* go to next char in array . . . */
              ++index;
            }
     return (index);
    }

/* function getline gets a line of input from standard */
/* input character by character, and continues until  */
/* EOF or a carriage return is encountered.            */
getline (dataline, limit)
char dataline[];
int limit;
    { int c, i;
        /* use getchar primitive to acquire c and assign c */
        /* to array element in dataline . . .              */
        for (i=0; i<limit-1 && (c=getchar()) != EOF && c != '\n'; ++i)
            dataline[i] = c;
        /* if carriage return is found, add the standard */
        /* C end-of-line char . . .                      */
        if (c == '\n')
          { dataline[i] = c;
              ++i;
          }
        dataline[i] = '\0';
        return (i);
    }
```

The code is easy to follow, with the possible exception of the details of parameter passing. The function "getline" is called from the main routine with the parameter "inputline." The function "getline" provides for the acquisition of a line from the keyboard. The array "dataline" is filled, character by character, by the C input primitive **getchar**. When either a newline character or the end-of-file marker or the limit of 255 characters is reached, the input is terminated, and the array is passed back to "inputline" in the main routine. Then the main routine calls the function "ltou" and passes the parameter "inputline." The function "ltou" then converts the string array, character by character, to uppercase and displays the result.

EXERCISES

1. Given the following Pascal code, write the corresponding C code.

   a.
   ```
   procedure findbigger (a,b:integer);
   var c: integer;
   begin
     if (a > b)
       then c:= a
       else c := b;
     if (a<>b)
       then writeln ('larger value is ',c)
       else writeln ('two numbers are equal');
   end;
   ```

   b.
   ```
   function average (a,b,c : integer) : real;
   begin
     average := (a+b+c)/3;
     writeln ('the average is ',average:5:2);
   end;
   ```
2. Write a C program using appropriate functions that inputs a series of integers, prints the unsorted list, sorts the list, and prints the sorted list. It should also print the high, low, and average values.
3. Write a grading program that inputs a series of student names and scores, assigns letter grades, and outputs a list of names and grades. Make any reasonable assumptions required to complete the program.
4. Write a C program containing a recursive function call to calculate factorial values. The user will input an integer between 1 and 10. The program should check for valid input (why?) and then output the appropriate factorial value.
5. Write a program using appropriate functions to count the number of lines in a file and print out the result.
6. Write a program using appropriate functions to count the number of words in a file and print out the result.

7. Write a program using appropriate functions that inputs a line of characters from standard input and prints out the line in uppercase, regardless of the case of the input characters.
8. Write a program using appropriate functions to copy the contents of a file to a new file with a different name. Prompt the user to get the name of the new file.

CHAPTER 9

Pointers, Records, and Structures

OVERVIEW OF POINTERS AND RECORDS

In addition to the features we have already described, both Pascal and C provide for the creation of elegant dynamic data structures by using pointer variables.

A **dynamic data structure** is a collection of information-containing elements. In Pascal, the elements of a dynamic data structure are called **records**; in C, they are called **structures**. The internal structure of each of these elements may be very simple or very complex. Each element is generally a collection of variable values, and at least one of these variables is a special type called a **pointer variable**. The component elements of a dynamic data structure occupy discrete memory locations (or **nodes**), and pointer variables provide a mechanism for linking the nodes together (Figure 9.1).

Pointer variables in Pascal and C will let you directly address memory locations and are the key to the construction of dynamic data structures. Pointers can be used to access each element of a dynamic data structure, and they provide the necessary links between nodes. Each record (or structure) generally contains a pointer variable that "points to" related nodes.

Dynamic data structures are dynamic—that is, they can change during program execution. An array in Pascal is a static data structure; at run-time the memory required for an array is allocated, and the structure remains static while the program is executed. A dynamic data structure can grow or shrink as the program executes. As required, new nodes can be created for new records, existing nodes can be deleted from the structure, and pointer variables can be adjusted to reflect changing relationships among the nodes.

FIGURE 9.1 As an alternative to arrays, data can be stored in memory nodes. These nodes can be joined by pointers to form a linked list, as shown in this schematic diagram.

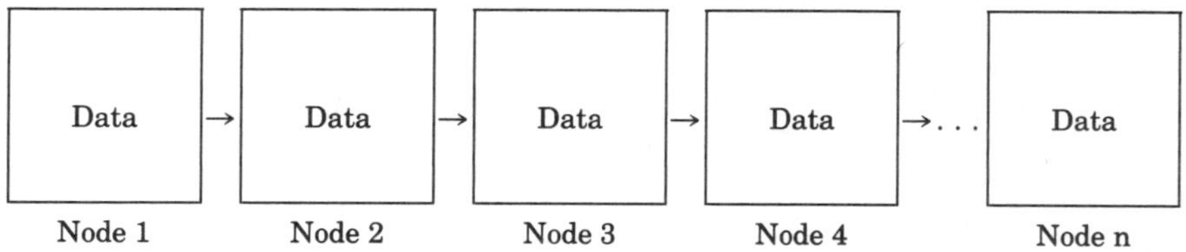

Pointer variables and dynamic data structures in Pascal are handled differently in different dialects of Pascal. When a new node is created in Pascal, some special command must be used to allocate the required memory space. In some versions of Pascal, this is accomplished by using the **new** command. When a node is deleted from the structure, the memory locations are usually deallocated; in some versions of Pascal, this is accomplished by using the **dispose** command. The declaration of pointer variables may also vary among dialects, as may the notation used for indicating pointers. Since C has much less variation in its implementations, there is also less variation in syntax and notation.

RECORDS AND STRUCTURES

Both C and Pascal include simple variables as a way of storing information and include arrays as a way of grouping variables together. They also include the concept of a **record**, which is a data structure that is a collection of variable values. A record can be a complex structure, containing values for a number of related variables, with each of these variables called a **field** within the record (see Figure 9.2).

Records in Pascal must have their structure defined in the type-declaration section at the beginning of the main program, procedure, or function in which they will be used. The general syntax for declaring a Pascal record is as follows:

```
type
    ⟨record-name⟩ = record
                        ⟨field 1⟩ : ⟨type⟩;
                        ⟨field 2⟩ : ⟨type⟩;
                    . . . ⟨field n⟩ : ⟨type⟩
                    end;
```

FIGURE 9.2 Each memory node can store several pieces of data (fields), and one field can be a pointer that points to the location of the next node on the list. In Pascal, each node corresponds to a record; in C, each node corresponds to a structure.

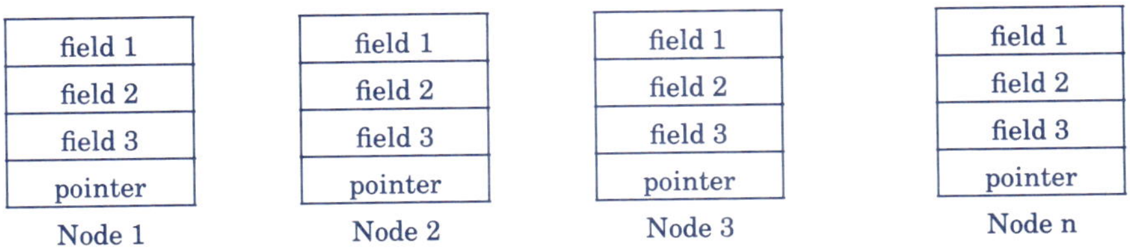

Once the record type has been defined, then variables can be declared to be of that type. For instance, you might declare a record to store student information. The record-name might be student, and the fields within the record might be student identification number, two test grades, and a final average.

To define such a record in Pascal and declare a variable of that record type, you would write the following:

```
type
     student = record
                    idnumber : integer;
                    firstgrade : integer;
                    secondgrade : integer;
                    average : real;
                end;
var
     firststudent : student;
```

A variable such as "firststudent" has been declared to have a specific structure. It actually has four values associated with it: an idnumber, two grade values, and an average value. Values can be assigned to those fields in several ways.

First, values can be assigned by using distinct assignment statements. For instance, the lines

```
firststudent.idnumber := 9999;
firststudent.firstgrade := 89;
firststudent.secondgrade := 91;
firststudent.average := 90.0;
```

will assign values to the fields within the specific record named "firststudent."

Alternatively, Pascal provides the **with** statement for placing values in record fields. The statement lines

```
with firststudent do
    begin
    idnumber := 9999;
    firstgrade := 89;
    secondgrade := 91;
    average := 90.0;
    end;
```

will accomplish the same result as the four assignment statements shown above.

The equivalent data structure in C is called a **structure**. As with Pascal records, a **structure** in C is a collection of variable values. The individual variables within a C structure are called **members**, and the name of the structure is called the **structure tag**. Structures in C are declared in generally the same way that records are in Pascal. The syntax of the C structure definition follows:

```
struct ⟨structure tag⟩
   {
   ⟨type⟩ ⟨variable 1⟩;
   ⟨type⟩ ⟨variable 2⟩;
    . . . ⟨type⟩ ⟨variable n⟩;
   };
```

Once a structure is defined, then variables can be specified to be of that type. The structure tag can be used in a variable type-declaration statement, just as if it were a predefined type; the only additional requirement is that the structure tag must be preceded by the word *structure* in the variable type-declaration statement.

For example, to declare the C equivalent of our Pascal student record, we would have to use the following statements:

```
struct student
   {
     int idnumber;
     int firstgrade;
     int secondgrade;
     float average;
   };

struct student firststudent;
```

The variable "firststudent" is declared to be of type student; since student is a structure, the structure tag "student" must be preceded by the word *struct* on the type-declaration line.

C also provides a quicker way of accomplishing the same goal. You can combine the structure definition with the declaration of variables that will have that type using the following syntax:

```
struct student
    {
      int idnumber;
      int firstgrade;
      int secondgrade;
      float average;
    } firststudent;
```

Since the variable name "firststudent" follows the closing brace of the structure definition, it is declared to be of type student. Any structure definition can be followed by a list of variable names (separated by commas), and those variables will automatically be declared to be of that type.

Values can be assigned to the members of a C structure in a manner similar to field assignments in Pascal. The following code would assign values to the members of the structure named "firststudent":

```
firststudent.idnumber = 9999;
firststudent.firstgrade = 89;
firststudent.secondgrade = 91;
firststudent.average = 90.0;
```

C also provides a means by which the values of a variable structure can be initialized at the time the variable is declared. The following code will declare the variable "firststudent" to be of type "student," and it will initialize the values of the members at the same time:

```
struct student firststudent = {9999, 89, 91, 90.0};
```

The syntax of record declaration in Pascal and structure declaration in C is summarized in Figure 9.3, and a short example illustrating the use of records and structures can be found in Figure 9.4

POINTERS IN PASCAL

Pointer variables are special. Most variables store values that are specified by the programmer or the user. Pointer variables, on the other hand, contain values that are not only not specified by the user or programmer, but that are often inaccessible as well. Pointer variables store the addresses of other variables, and many implementations of pointer variables will either not permit these values to be printed or will print out meaningless values.

The use of pointers in Pascal involves a number of distinct problems. These include: (1) the proper declaration of pointer variables in the header sections of a main program, procedure, or function; (2) the assignment of values to the pointer variables; and (3) using pointers to create dynamic data structures.

Declaring pointer variables in Pascal resembles the declaration of other variable types, but with several differences. For instance, a special notation

FIGURE 9.3 General declaration of records in Pascal and structures in C.

Pascal:

```
⟨recordname⟩ = record
                   ⟨field1 name⟩ : ⟨type⟩;
                   ⟨field2 name⟩ : ⟨type⟩;
                   ⟨field3 name⟩ : ⟨type⟩;

                   ⟨fieldn name⟩ : ⟨type⟩;
               end;
```

C:

```
struct ⟨structure-tag⟩
    {
        ⟨type⟩ ⟨field1 name⟩;
        ⟨type⟩ ⟨field2 name⟩;
        ⟨type⟩ ⟨field3 name⟩;

        ⟨type⟩ ⟨fieldn name⟩;
    }⟨variable name being declared⟩;
```

must be used in some contexts to indicate that a variable is a pointer. This notation varies with different dialects of Pascal; for the sake of our discussion, a pointer variable will often be associated with an up-arrow (^) to indicate its special status. Following this convention, the declaration of a pointer variable in Pascal might look like this:

```
type
    ⟨node-type⟩ = record
                      ⟨field contents⟩;
                  end;

    ⟨pointer-type⟩ = ^⟨node-type⟩;
var
    ⟨pointer-name⟩ : ⟨pointer-type⟩;
```

This set of declarations has several parts. First, there is the declaration of a record structure. Second, there is the declaration of a pointer-type, which is able to point to that type of record structure (that is, it can store the memory address of that type of record). Third, there is the declaration of a variable that is of that specific pointer type.

How might this be specifically applied? Let's rewrite the declarations of our student record code in the last section using the pointer format.

FIGURE 9.4 Example of declaration of records in Pascal and structures in C.

Pascal:

```
type
   student = record
                idnumber : integer;
                grade1   : integer;
                grade2   : integer;
                final    : integer;
                average  : real;
                grade    : char;
                end;

var
     firststudent : student;
```

C:

```
structure student
     {
            int idnumber;
            int grade1;
            int grade2;
            int final;
            float average;
            char grade;
     }    firststudent;
```

```
type
     student = record
                 idnumber : integer;
                 firstgrade : integer;
                 secondgrade : integer;
                 average : real;
               end;

     studentpointer = ^student;

var
     classmember : studentpointer;
```

Assuming that this code declares the pointer variables correctly, how then can they be used properly? How is the record node created and how is it accessed to assign values to fields or read values from fields? A node is created in most Pascal implementations by using the **new** statement (or a similar construct). Once the node is created, then fields within the record are accessed in a manner very similar to our previous example. For example, the following code will create a new node and assign field values to that node:

```
new (classmember);

classmember^.idnumber := 9999;
classmember^.firstgrade := 89;
classmember^.secondgrade := 91;
classmember^.average := 90.0;
```

Pointers can be used to create elegant, complex data structures. The key to most of these structures is the inclusion of at least one pointer variable as a field within a record. This will let one node in a structure contain information that points to another node. Let's modify our student record structure by adding another field; this additional field will be a pointer variable, and it will allow us to link student nodes together in a list. *This linked-list structure can be the basic foundation of stacks, queues, trees, and a host of other data structures, although a discussion of those structures is beyond the scope of this book.*

```
type
     student = record
                    idnumber : integer;
                    firstgrade : integer;
                    secondgrade : integer;
                    average : real;
                    nextstudent : studentpointer;
               end;

     studentpointer = ^student;
var
     classmember : studentpointer;
     anotherclassmember : studentpointer;
```

These statements declare that the record now contains an additional field, a pointer variable named "nextstudent" that can store the address of another variable. What kind of variable? Since it is of type studentpointer, it can store the address of another student record node. The following code will create two nodes and link them together:

```
(*This creates two student record nodes.*)
(*Pointer classmember points to first node.*)
(*Pointer anotherclassmember points to second*.)
     new (classmember);
     new (anotherclassmember);
```

```
(*Now make first node point to second node . . . *)
    classmember^.nextstudent := anotherclassmember;
```

The first node that was created now contains the information needed to find the second node. Similarly, it would be possible to create a large number of such nodes, with each node containing a pointer variable storing information about where the next node on the list could be found. A set of these nodes, with each node pointing to another node somewhere in memory, is called a **linked list**.

From this example, it should be obvious that pointers in Pascal can be assigned values in one of two ways. A value is assigned to a pointer when the **new** statement is executed; a node is created, and the address of that node is assigned to the pointer. A value can also be assigned using a traditional assignment statement; if one pointer has a value, then a second pointer can be assigned the same value by setting the second pointer equal to the first pointer.

POINTERS IN C

C pointers provide their own special problems. Since C is primarily a systems-programming language, directly accessing and manipulating memory addresses is one of C's basic concerns. Therefore, using pointer variables is an important part of C, and C provides more pointer-related operations (including pointer arithmetic) than Pascal does. Some C programs may use pointers heavily, however, and this may present problems. The combination of C's natural conciseness and the indirection inherent in pointer variables often produces programs that are breathtakingly unreadable.

With this in mind, we will introduce the basic concepts necessary to using pointers in C, and we will not attempt to cover advanced applications. The discussion will be limited to the declaration of pointers, the assignment of values to pointers, and the use of pointers to create lists. *We will also cover the use of C pointers in parameter lists in the next section. As we will see, the use of pointers can provide the equivalent of Pascal* **call by reference** *function calls.*

The declaration of pointer variables in C is again similar to the usual variable-type declarations. As in Pascal, a distinct notation must be adopted to use with pointer variables. This notation will not, however, involve the use of up-arrows. Instead, it involves the use of two new operators.

In C, there are two operators that are used extensively in association with pointers. The first operator is symbolized by *. When a pointer variable is preceded by *, then the expression evaluates to the contents of whatever the pointer is pointing to. For instance, if a pointer named p is pointing to a memory location storing the integer 15, then *p evaluates to 15.

The second operator that is used extensively is symbolized by &. When any variable is preceded by &, then that expression evaluates to the address at which the variable is stored. You can think of the & operator as extracting the location of variables. Once those addresses are known, they can be assigned to a pointer variable. For instance, if there is an int variable named q and a pointer variable named p, then the pointer can be assigned the address of q by simply saying "p = &q".

Declaring C pointer variables involves using the * prefix. To continue with the example of our student record structure, the code we considered earlier could be rewritten using the pointer format in the following way:

```
struct student
{
     int idnumber;
     int firstgrade;
     int secondgrade;
     float average;
};
struct student *classmember;
```

These declarations specify that the variable "classmember" is a pointer and that it is able to point to a structure of type student.

How is space dynamically allocated for this structure within the program? The C library generally contains a special function, **alloc()**, dedicated to this purpose, and its use is similar to the analogous **new** function in Pascal. The specific use of this function will vary with each compiler, but generally the syntax is as follows:

```
classmember = alloc();
```

This function will create the structure node in memory and place its address in the variable "classmember."

Once the node is created, its members can be assigned values. The assignment of values to members in a C structure is similar to assignment of values to Pascal record fields. The following code assigns values to the members of our student structure:

```
(*classmember).idnumber = 9999;
(*classmember).firstgrade = 89;
(*classmember).secondgrade = 91;
(*classmember).average = 90.0;
```

The parentheses are required in these statements because the * is really a unary operator, and the parentheses are needed for enforcing the correct order of operations.

In addition to the previous type of assignment statement, values can be assigned to members of a structure by a second kind of notation. The notation "→" can be used to specify one member of a structure. For instance, the term "classmember→idnumber" refers to the member named "idnumber" that is a part of the structure named "classmember." This notation permits easy assignment of values to the members of a structure. The following statements are equivalent to the previous statements:

```
classmember→idnumber = 9999;
classmember→firstgrade = 89;
classmember→secondgrade = 91;
classmember→average = 90.0;
```

The use of this "→" notation is somewhat easier to read for many programmers, and it is very common.

How can pointers in C be used to construct a linked list analogous to the data structure that we constructed in Pascal? First, you must declare the appropriate structure, with one of the members of the structure defined to be a pointer variable. The appropriate declarations might look like this:

```
struct student
  {
    int idnumber;
    int firstgrade;
    int secondgrade;
    float average;
    struct student *r;
  };

struct student *p,*q;
```

Now, what kind of statement would be needed to link together two nodes? In C, linking together those two nodes in memory requires only a single statement:

```
p→r = q;
```

This statement can be interpreted as meaning: Look at the structure in memory pointed to by the pointer p. One member of that structure is the pointer r. Assign to that variable the value of the pointer q.

A linked list of many such nodes can be easily constructed in a similar way. Each node can contain a structure, one member of which is a pointer. The member that is a pointer can contain the address of some related node on the list.

Figure 9.5 illustrates the declaration of structures in C and the assignment of values to structure members.

USING POINTERS IN C PARAMETER LISTS: CALL BY REFERENCE

When we discussed C function calls in Chapter 8, we noted that functions in C may only be **called by value**. That is, when a function is called, the calling

FIGURE 9.5 Sample program illustrating use of structures in C.

```
#include ⟨stdio.h⟩

struct datanode
    {     int firstvalue;
          int secondvalue;
          struct datanode *nextnode;
    };
struct datanode *node;

/*main: assign values to demonstration node*/
main()
{ int firstnumber, secondnumber; /*local variables*/

printf ("Input an integer: \n");
scanf ("%d", &firstnumber);
printf ("Input another integer: \n");
scanf ("%d", &secondnumber);

/* allocate space for node */
/* analogous to Pascal NEW */
    node = alloc();

/*alternative ways to assign field values to structure*/
(*node).firstvalue = firstnumber;
node->secondvalue = secondnumber;

}
```

statement passes the values of the actual parameters to the formal parameter list variables. Whatever happens to those values or to the formal parameter variables within the body of the function has no effect on the original actual parameter variables or their values.

We have also mentioned that there is a single exception to this rule—when arrays are passed as parameters, the effect is to call the function **by reference**. *Whatever happens to the array on the formal parameter list is reflected in the array that was on the actual parameter list. The reason for this will become clear shortly.*

In some situations, however, it is desirable or even necessary to call a function **by reference**. It might be desirable to have changes in a formal parameter variable reflected in the original actual parameter variable. C does provide a means by which **call by reference** can be accomplished. This is done by directly passing the addresses of actual parameters to their corresponding formal parameters. Passing the addresses of the actual parameters will make it necessary to use the & operator introduced earlier. The & is a unary operator that precedes a variable name and returns the address of that variable. The following code is an example of how to call a function by reference in C:

```
#include <stdio.h>
  int a,b;

doublerfunction ( p )
  int *p;  /* declares p is pointer to int*/
  {
    *p = (*p) + (*p);
    return ();
  }

/* main */
main ()
  {
    a = 4;
    b = doublerfunction (&a);
  }
```

This function will initialize the variable a to the value 4, and then call the function "doublerfunction." Look at the actual parameter used in the function call. What is passed to the function is not the *value* of the variable a, but the *address* of variable a. Now look at the formal parameter on the function header line. The formal parameter is a pointer, which receives the address of the actual parameter. The function code itself is trivial; the contents of the address pointed to by pointer p is doubled. When control is returned to the main function, however, the value of variable a has been changed by the function call. In effect, the function has been **called by reference**. A typical C program that illustrates parameter passing by reference is shown in Figure 9.6.

We noted earlier that when an array is passed as a parameter to a function, the function is called by reference. The reason for this is simple: when an array name is passed as an actual parameter, what is passed to the function is the address of the zero-eth element of the array. Thus, when arrays are passed, an address is being passed implicitly, with no further programmer effort.

POINTER ARITHMETIC IN C

When a Pascal program uses a pointer, the actual value of the pointer is usually either meaningless or inaccessible. In C, however, the values of pointers can (and often are) manipulated. Manipulating pointer values can often increase the efficiency of execution, since you are dealing with values that are one level closer to the machine.

For instance, consider the following situation. You have stored 100 data

FIGURE 9.6 Sample program which illustrates pointers and passing parameters by reference in C.

```
#include <stdio.h>
/* this demonstrates use of functions */
/* and passing parameters by reference */

/*function to return user input value*/
int getvalue ()
{ int inputvalue;
  /* get an integer value from user at standard input */
  printf ("Input a value: ");
  scanf ("%d",&inputvalue);
  printf ("Inputvalue: %d\n",inputvalue);
  /*return value for function name*/
  return(inputvalue);
}/*end function getvalue */

/*function to swap values*/
int swap (firstnumber, secondnumber)
int *firstnumber, *secondnumber;
{
  int tempstorage;
  printf ("Original order: %d   %d\n",*firstnumber, *secondnumber);
  tempstorage = *firstnumber;
  *firstnumber = *secondnumber;
  *secondnumber = tempstorage;

  printf ("Swapped order: %d   %d\n",*firstnumber,*secondnumber);

  /*return no value for function name*/
  return;
}

/*main: get two numbers from user and swap values */
main()
{ int firstvalue, secondvalue;

  firstvalue = getvalue();
  secondvalue = getvalue();
  printf ("Firstvalue: %d     Secondvalue:     %d\n",firstvalue,secondvalue);

  swap (&firstvalue,&secondvalue);
}
```

items in an array (which are stored in a contiguous block of memory), and you want to access those 100 elements. There are several ways of doing that.

One approach might be to assign the values of the array elements to a variable:

```
int a, index;
int array[100];

⟨code to assign values to array[0] through array[99]⟩

for (index=0; index<=99; ++index)
     {
     a = array[index];
     printf ("array element %d = %d\n",index,a);
     }
```

A second approach would involve the use of pointers and pointer arithmetic. If we assign the memory location of the first element of the array to a pointer, we can access the rest of the array by simply incrementing the pointer value and asking for the contents of the current pointer location. This code will execute more quickly than the previous code, since we are operating closer to the machine level:

```
int a;
int *p;  /* declare pointer p, points to integer */
int array [100];

⟨code to assign values to array[0] through array[99]⟩

/* assign location of array to p */
p = &array[0];

for (index=0; index <= 99); ++index)
     {
     a = *p;  /* assign a contents of p */
     printf ("array element %d = %d\n", index, a);
     ++p;  /* increment p, point to next location*/
     }
```

Note that within the loop code the operation "++p" is perfectly legal. The value of p is incremented, and the pointer now points to the next location in memory. This operation will permit direct access to the array contents, without referencing the array name and adding that layer of execution to the code.

Just as pointer values can be incremented, they can be decremented as well. Pointer values can also be assigned the results of expressions that involve pointer arithmetic. For example, if a second pointer, called p2, had been declared in our example above, then p2 = ++p is a legal statement; this would take the address to which p points and assign to p2 the following address.

C SOFTWARE TOOLS: CREATING A LINKED LIST IN C

The linked list is an essential tool in Pascal. With a linked list available, it is possible to build and maintain important data structures such as stacks, queues, and trees. Such a capability is also extremely important in C, and Figure 9.7 presents a program that creates a linked list in C. This program will create a list of students. Each student is represented by a structure containing an identification number, a series of test scores, and a final letter grade. The student structures are linked by a pointer field in the structures. An initial pointer, "class" points to the first student's structure, and the final structure points to nil to end the list. Items 6 and 9 in the following exercises suggest further modifications that could be made to this program.

FIGURE 9.7 C program that creates a linked list of structures to store student data. When a value of 0 is entered for idnumber, the id numbers of students currently in the list are displayed.

```
#include <stdio.h>
#define NIL 0

struct studentnode
    {int idnumber;
     int firstgrade;
     int secondgrade;
     int finalexam;
     char coursegrade;
     struct studentnode *nextnode
    };

struct studentnode *firstnode, *oldnode, *newnode;
struct studentnode *printnode;

int id, score1, score2, final;
int average;
char letter;

/* main function creates first student node, then */
/* continues to add nodes to list until zero is */
/* entered for idnumber. list of idnumbers is then */
/* printed out. */

main()
  {
     /* create first node using C library function 'alloc' */
     /* which is similar to Pascal's 'new' statement. */
```

```
        /* then record that node permanently in 'firstnode'. */
        oldnode = alloc();
        firstnode = oldnode;

        /* get input for the first node and record it */
        id = getdata();
        oldnode->idnumber = id;
        oldnode->firstgrade = score1;
        oldnode->secondgrade = score2;
        oldnode->finalexam = final;
        oldnode->coursegrade = letter;
        oldnode->nextnode = NIL;

        /* repeat, adding nodes until zero is entered for id */
        while ((id = getdata()) != 0)
            { newnode = alloc();
              newnode->idnumber = id;
              newnode->firstgrade = score1;
              newnode->secondgrade = score2;
              newnode->finalexam = final;
              newnode->coursegrade = letter;
              newnode->nextnode = NIL;

              /*link previous node to the new node*/
              oldnode->nextnode = &newnode;
              /* reset oldnode to point to this current node */
              oldnode = newnode;
            }

        /* print out idnumbers when list is entered */

        /* start at the beginning of the list . . . */
        printnode = firstnode;
        printf ("Here a list of student id numbers: \n");

        /* and go down the list until NIL is found.*/
        while (printnode->nextnode != NIL)
            { printf ("%d\n", printnode->idnumber);
              printnode = printnode->nextnode;
            }
    } /* end of main function */

    /* function getdata reads input for data to record about */
    /* each student and assigns letter grades */
    int getdata ()
        {
           printf ("Enter student id: "); scanf ("%d\n", &id);
           printf ("Enter first test: "); scanf ("%d\n", &score1);
           printf ("Enter second test: "); scanf("%d\n", &score2);
           printf ("Enter final exam: "); scanf ("%d\n", &final);
```

FIGURE 9.7 (Continued)

```
        average = (score1 + score2 +2*final)/4;

        if (average > 90) letter = 'A';
          else if (average > 80) letter = 'B';
          else if (average > 70) letter = 'C';
          else if (average > 60) letter = 'D';
          else letter = 'F';
        return (id);
    }
```

EXERCISES

1. Given the following Pascal code, write the corresponding C code.

   a.
   ```
   type
     string = array [1. .20] of char;
     airlineflight = record
                       flightnum : integer;
                       numseats : integer;
                       pilot : string;
                       origin : string;
                       destination : string;
                       end;
     var flight: airlineflight;
   ```

   b.
   ```
   type
     string = array [1. .20] of char;
     dog = record
             breed : string;
             sex : boolean;
             color : string;
             regisnum : integer;
             name : string;
             end;
   ```

   c.
   ```
   with dog do
     begin
     breed := "beagle";
     color := "spotted";
     name := "Snoopy";
     end;
   ```

   d.
   ```
   flight.flightnum := 999;
   flight.numseats := 152;
   flight.pilot := "Jones";
   flight.origin := "Atlanta";
   ```

2. Write a C program that inputs ten numbers from the keyboard and stores them in a linked list.
3. Write a C program that inputs ten numbers, stores them in a linked list, sorts them, and prints out the sorted list. Use a sort algorithm of your choice.
4. Write a C program that inputs a list of ten integers and stores them in a linked list. Then input a key value from the keyboard and search the list for that key value. Print an appropriate message if the key is present in the list.
5. Write a program that inputs a list of ten integers and stores them in a linked list. Then input a key value from the keyboard; if that value is already present in the list, delete it from the list.
6. Examine the demonstration program, "student-ist," provided in Figure 9.7. Modify the program so that it prompts the user for a new identification number. Search the list. If the number is already present, report that fact with an appropriate message. If the number isn't present, get the required information and add the new student to the list.
7. Modify the program written in Exercise 6, so that the list is maintained in sorted order at all times.
8. Modify the program written in Exercise 6, so that the user may delete a specified student from the list at any time.
9. Modify the program written in Exercise 6, so that the user is presented with a menu of options, each of which can be exercised. The menu should let the user:

    a. add student records
    b. modify student records
    c. delete student records
    d. print out individual records
    e. print out all student records

    Any other desirable options may be added.

CHAPTER 10

Using C under UNIX

INTRODUCTION

C is currently available for use on many machines. Although it has been primarily implemented on minicomputers, the language has become increasingly available on microcomputers in recent years. Probably the most common host machines for C, however, are the DEC PDP-11 and VAX series, and UNIX is the most common operating system under which C programs are written and executed.

This chapter will briefly introduce you to the UNIX operating system and to the procedures by which C programs are constructed under UNIX. The UNIX system is currently so complex that this chapter can only serve as a brief overview of a few UNIX operations. If you are using UNIX already, this chapter will provide a context within which you can view C operations. If you are not using UNIX, this chapter will provide you with an introduction to the system.

Although UNIX is too large to be implemented on most microcomputers, operating systems that are functional subsets of UNIX are available for those systems. *Operating systems such as UNICA, XENIX and IDRIS are examples of these.* The information in this chapter will summarize operations under UNIX, but many of the same commands will be used with these micro UNIX look-alikes.

THE UNIX OPERATING SYSTEM

UNIX is a unique operating system that is at once simple and complex. It began as a single-user operating system, allowing only one person to use the computer at a time. It was soon expanded to a time-sharing system, allowing several people to share the computing resources of a single machine. More recently, with the increasing use of more powerful microcomputers, UNIX and its related functional subsets have once again returned as powerful single-user operating systems. With the introduction of microcomputers containing microprocessors such as the Motorola 68000, the implementation of full UNIX on microcomputers is now possible.

UNIX itself has several components in its structure. At the heart of the operating system is the **kernel**, the central code that is machine independent and that defines most of the UNIX basic functions. In addition to this kernel, more code is introduced at this level when UNIX is implemented on a specific machine to handle machine-dependent functions, such as I/O.

Above this kernel of code is the **shell**. The shell consists of code that serves as a command interpreter; when the user enters a UNIX command, the shell interprets it and serves as the necessary interface to the underlying kernel code.

In addition to this central code, a full UNIX implementation includes a set of interlocking programs. These programs provide a complete programming environment for the UNIX programmer. This collection of programs includes utility programs, such as **sort** and **diff**. **Sort** *will sort a file that is specified as an input parameter.* **Diff** *will take two files as input parameters, compare the files, and output any differences between them.* It also includes editors, formatting programs, and electronic mail. Most important for our purposes, it also includes a C compiler.

THE UNIX SHELL

UNIX is an interactive operating system—the user enters commands from a terminal, and the system gives back responses. The shell is the part of the UNIX code that provides for this interaction. It permits the user to issue instructions to UNIX and have the instructions executed properly.

The UNIX shell, like every part of UNIX, is written in C. It is a program that serves as a command interpreter. It reads the instructions given to it, determines what they mean, and then attempts to carry them out. These commands can come either from a person typing them at a keyboard or from a file containing a series of commands previously entered. Such a file is called a **shell procedure**.

When you log on to a UNIX system, the shell indicates its readiness to respond to you by printing a prompt. The default prompt for UNIX is the % symbol. *As with most elements of a UNIX environment, however, this is under user control. It is possible to reset the prompt to any character or string of characters.* Once the prompt is printed, the user can issue any UNIX command. A UNIX command is really the name of a program that is available on the system. When a command is entered, the shell finds and executes the specified program. For example, if the user enters after the prompt

```
% date
```

the shell will find the program **date**, execute it, and print the following information on the terminal:

```
Fri Jul 1 9:12:47 1985
```

Date is one of the many system utilities available under UNIX. *Typing* **date** *when you want to know the time is characteristic of UNIX's idiosyncrasies.*

STANDARD INPUT AND OUTPUT IN UNIX

UNIX bases many of its operations on the concept of a **standard input** and **standard output**. Standard input is the default source of information when a program is executed, and this source is defined when the system is implemented on a given machine. In most (if not all) implementations, standard input is defined to be the keyboard. Similarly, standard output is defined to be the default device to which output is directed. On most machines, standard output will be the user's display device (screen or printer).

If no other source of input is specified when a program is run, the program will expect input from standard input; that is, it will wait for required data to be entered at the keyboard. Likewise, if no other file or device is specified when a program is run, any output will be directed to the user's display device.

When the user provides input information to a program from the keyboard, the program will accept that information just as if it were reading from a file. The program will wait for the user to finish inputting information, and then it will process the information. *The user must terminate the input with CONTROL-D, which is the standard end-of-file flag in UNIX.*

COMMAND LINE ARGUMENTS

When you issue a command (such as **date**) in UNIX, you are really invoking some specific system program. Some of these system programs can be called without passing any parameters to them. Other system commands, however, can be called and passed arguments at the same time.

For instance, another system command is **sort**. This command will sort any file provided to it as input. The required input could be provided directly from the keyboard (standard input); if the user typed **sort**, followed by a list of items terminated by a CONTROL-D, then the sorted list would be printed on the standard output.

This command could also be followed by a filename, which would cause the command to use the specified file for input, instead of standard input. A typical use would be

```
% sort ⟨filename⟩
```

When the command is executed, the contents of the specified file will be sorted and the result printed on the standard output.

Other system commands may require two or more arguments. For instance, the system command **diff** requires two arguments, so when it is invoked two filenames might be provided for input. A typical call would be:

```
% diff ⟨filename1⟩ ⟨filename2⟩
```

When this command is executed, the differences between the two files will be printed on the standard output.

REDIRECTING INPUT AND OUTPUT UNDER UNIX

If no other output has been specified, the output will be printed out on the user's display device (standard output). However, it is possible to direct output to another device or file using the > symbol. For instance, if you want to sort the contents of a file named "inputfile" and save the results in a file named "outputfile," an appropriate UNIX command would be:

```
% sort inputfile > outputfile
```

There are also several other ways of accomplishing this under UNIX.

We've seen how the output of a program can be directed to the standard output and how it can be redirected to a file. It is also possible to direct the output from one program straight into a second program, where it can be used as input. This kind of redirection is called a **pipe** and can be accomplished using the | UNIX operator.

For instance, suppose the program "prog1" generated a list of names from an input data file named "inputlist." The command

```
% prog1 inputlist | sort
```

would take the data from "inputlist" as input, execute "prog1" using that data, and then take the output from that program and send it to the system program **sort**. **Sort** would then sort the list of names and print the result on the standard output. Likewise, the command line

```
% prog1 inputlist | sort > outputfile
```

would save the sorted list in the file named "outputfile."

COMMAND OPTIONS

Many UNIX shell commands have a variety of options that can be specified at the time of execution. These options vary with each command, and a fuller explanation is not possible here.

In general, if an option will be used, it must be specified on the command line between the command name and the command's argument list. An option is specified by following the command name with a blank space, a dash, and one or more characters. For instance, the command line

```
% sort -r inputfile
```

causes the **sort** program to sort the contents of "inputfile" in reverse order, since the shell command **sort** is followed by the **reverse** option (−r).

OVERVIEW: CREATING AND EXECUTING A C PROGRAM

When you create and execute a C program under UNIX, there are three distinct processes involved. These three processes are

1. Creating the C source code using an editor.
2. Compiling the source code into executable code.
3. Executing the compiled code.

The following three sections will explore these processes in more detail. The UNIX environment contains several editors that can be used to create text files. Any of these can be used to create a C source file, and the next section will discuss several options. After that we will discuss how to compile this C source file into an executable file, and the third section will explain how to run this executable file under UNIX.

USING THE UNIX EDITORS TO CREATE A C SOURCE FILE

A C source program is initially created as a text file under UNIX. The means by which this text file is created is largely irrelevant, and any convenient editor can be used to generate this source file. The only restriction that must be observed is that the name of the text file must be of the form

```
⟨filename⟩.c
```

The name of a C source program must end in ".c". Except for that restriction, the source file can have any name valid for your system.

Under UNIX there are usually at least two text editors available. The first, **ed**, is a line-oriented editor that can be used effectively on any display device (including a hardcopy device). The second, **vi**, is an editor oriented for use on a video terminal. *For those familiar with other editors,* **ed** *is similar to the DEC editor TECO or the CP/M editor* **ed**, *and* **vi** *resembles TECO/VT.*

The editor **ed** is a line-oriented editor and intended primarily for use on printing terminals. Text is entered line by line, and editing commands require that the target lines be specified with each command. Editing is performed using an invisible pointer into the text file as a reference point, and commands to move this invisible pointer are available.

Ed is invoked (as usual under UNIX) by simply naming the program. The system command looks like this:

```
% ed <filename>.c
```

This command will invoke **ed** and open a text file named ⟨filename⟩.c. *If the file already exists, this command will permit you to edit it. If the file does not already exist, this command creates a new file.* Following this call, text can be entered and manipulated. Text is appended to the file by giving the command to enter append mode:

```
:a
```

Any text that is now entered will be appended to the file. When the desired text has been completed, the user enters CONTROL-D, which terminates the append mode. Then the commands "w" and "q" will, respectively, write the text to the file in your directory and quit the editor. A typical sequence of **ed** commands is seen in Figure 10.1.

The second editor commonly available under UNIX is **vi**. **Vi** provides a full-screen editor for use on video terminals. Under **vi**, your text is printed on the screen at all times, and the location of the cursor indicates your current location in the text. This editor is invoked by the following call:

```
% vi <filename>.c
```

The screen clears and text can then be entered into a new file or appended to an existing file. It is possible to move the cursor through the text, delete characters, move text, insert text, and perform other standard editing functions. The changes are effected directly on the screen, and when the required text has been entered, the command ":wq" will write the text to the file and quit the editor. A typical sequence of **vi** commands is shown in Figure 10.2.

Both **ed** and **vi** are full-function editors, and you should consult your sys-

FIGURE 10.1 Schematic of typical editing session with ***ed****.*

Command Sequence	Effect
% ed demoprogram.c	Invoke ed; create new file or load old file for editing.
:	The ed prompt
:a	Append text
⟨text entered⟩	
:wq	Write to file and quit the editor.
%	UNIX prompt returns.

FIGURE 10.2 Schematic of typical editing session with ***vi****.*

Command Sequence	Effect
% vi demoprogram.c	Creates new file named demo.c or loads existing file for editing. If new file, screen will clear. If old file, old text is displayed.
⟨enter text⟩	
⟨esc⟩ : wq	Escape places in command mode. ":wq" writes to file and quits editor.
%	UNIX prompt returns.

tem manuals for a complete description of the features and commands that are available on your specific system.

COMPILING C SOURCE PROGRAMS UNDER UNIX

The UNIX environment virtually always contains a C compiler, and it is easy to compile your source programs using this compiler.

Before compiling the C source file, however, it is good practice to use the program **lint** to detect possible syntax errors. **Lint** is called by entering

```
% lint ⟨filename⟩.c
```

In response, a detailed report of possible programming errors will be directed to standard output. *The output can be redirected to another file, using the methods described earlier.*

When you are ready to compile your program, you invoke the system C compiler by entering the shell command

```
% cc ⟨filename⟩.c
```

This command will invoke the C compiler, and the source file "⟨filename⟩.c" will be compiled. If no errors are detected, the executable code that is created will be saved in the file "a.out."

Several options are available for use with the **cc** command. The two most important options are the "–c" and "–o" options. The "–c" option will cause the executable code to be saved under the same filename as the original source code, except that ".o" will be added as a suffix. The suffix ".o" indicates that the file contains object code. For example, the shell command

```
% cc -c ⟨filename⟩.c
```

will compile the source code found in "⟨filename⟩.c" and save the compiled code with the name "⟨filename⟩.o".

The "−o" option is used for specifying that the executable code should be stored under some name other than "a.out" or the original filename. For example, if you want to save the executable code under another filename, the following shell command should be used:

```
% cc -o ⟨newfilename⟩ ⟨filename⟩.c
```

This command will compile the source code found in "⟨filename⟩.c" and save it in your directory under the name "⟨newfilename⟩.o". *Again, the ".o" suffix for the new filename indicates that this file contains object code.*

The **cc** command can be passed more than one filename as an argument, and the two options just discussed can also be used in those situations. For example, the shell command

```
% cc ⟨file1⟩.c ⟨file2⟩.c
```

will compile both source files and produce a single object file under the name "a.out." Since many C programs are written in distinct units linked together at compile-time, this is very common. In addition, the shell command

```
% cc -c ⟨file1⟩.c ⟨file2⟩.c
```

will compile both files and save the compiled files under the names "⟨file1⟩.o" and "⟨file2⟩.o." Similarly, the shell command

```
% cc -o ⟨newfilename⟩ ⟨file1⟩.c ⟨file2⟩.c
```

will compile the two source files and store the combined object code in the object file "⟨newfilename⟩.o."

EXECUTING C PROGRAMS UNDER UNIX

Executing C programs is simple under UNIX. Like all UNIX programs, a C program is executed by entering the name of the file containing executable code and providing any necessary arguments.

For example, if a source file named "demo.c" has been created and it requires no arguments for execution, the following sequence will compile and execute the program

```
% cc demo.c
% a.out
```

Since the **cc** command will save executable code under the name "a.out" unless otherwise instructed, the first line will compile the source code and save the compiled code, and the second line will execute the program.

If the program requires arguments (see the discussion of **argc** and **argv** in Chapter 8), then the sequence would be different:

```
% cc demo.c
% a.out ⟨argument1⟩ ⟨argument2⟩ . . .
```

The first line would compile the program and save the code under the name "a.out," and the second line would execute the compiled code. The necessary arguments are provided immediately after the name of the file containing the executable code.

Of course, if the "– c" or "– o" option has been used to save the compiled code under some name other than "a.out", then that name would be used instead of "a.out" in the above commands.

REFERENCING FILES FROM C PROGRAMS—UNIX COMMANDS

In this introduction to C, we have provided a survey of most of the important operations possible in the language. One very important topic that is somewhat beyond the scope of our discussion is file manipulation from within C programs. The precise procedures for opening, closing, writing to, and reading from files is system dependent, and we will provide only a general overview of the commands available.

There are two ways of manipulating files in C: via the operating system commands, or by using I/O routines available in the standard library. We will briefly look at these two methods, but you should refer to your system reference manuals for a more extensive discussion.

Generally, some special operating system commands would be available for manipulating files within C programs. UNIX includes the following:

creat—creates a new file
open—opens file for read/write operations
read—reads a specified number of bytes
write—writes a specified number of bytes
close—closes a file

The **creat** system call must be used to create new files before they can be used. The format for this system call is as follows:

```
creat (⟨arg1⟩, ⟨arg2⟩);
```

The two arguments passed to this system call are the name of the file and the mode in which it is being created. Possible modes are read, write, or read/write.

The **open** system call opens files that had been previously created and is often of the form:

```
open (⟨arg1⟩, ⟨arg2⟩, ⟨arg3⟩);
```

The three arguments that are passed to this system function are usually the name of the file, the mode for which it is being opened (read, write, or read/write), and the **file descriptor**. The file descriptor is an integer value that is returned by the **open** system call and that can be used for identifying the file in other operations.

The **read** system call is often of the form:

```
read (⟨arg1⟩, ⟨arg2⟩, ⟨arg3⟩);
```

The three arguments passed to the **read** system call are usually the file descriptor, the destination for the data read, and the number of bytes to be read. The destination for the data read is usually an array.

When reading a file, it is common to continue reading until an end-of-file, or EOF, marker is encountered. The exact nature of this EOF marker will vary with the system implementation. It may be a specific control-character or it may be some other special signal to mark the end of the file. Consult your system manual for details.

The **write** system call is used in a similar way. The system call looks like this:

```
write (⟨arg1⟩, ⟨arg2⟩, ⟨arg3⟩);
```

The three arguments in the **write** system call are the file-descriptor, the source from which the data being written can be obtained, and the number of bytes to write. The source of the data being written is often an array.

The **close** command is usually implemented in the form:

```
close (⟨arg1⟩);
```

in which the single argument necessary is the file descriptor.

These are UNIX system commands, but similar commands are usually available under other related systems.

REFERENCING FILES FROM C PROGRAMS—USE OF STANDARD LIBRARY ROUTINES

In addition to the above UNIX commands, the standard I/O library also includes routines that can be used to access files under most systems. These include:

fopen—opens a file
fprintf—prints formatted data to file
fscanf—reads formatted data from file
fclose—closes a file

These routines are somewhat different from the related UNIX system calls, and their use in programs requires different declarations. These calls depend on the definition of a structure called **file** in the standard library header file ⟨stdio.h⟩. Operations are conducted with respect to a file descriptor, but the type of this file descriptor is a pointer to this **file** structure. *In the UNIX system calls, the file descriptor is an integer.*

The syntax required for using the **fopen** function call is slightly complicated. First, the appropriate type declarations must be made, and then the function can be called later:

```
FILE *fopen (), fd;
     :
     :

fd = fopen (⟨filename⟩, ⟨mode⟩);
```

As in the UNIX system calls, there are three modes: read, write, and read/write. An important difference is that files need not be created before they are accessed. If a file that does not exist is opened, it is created and then opened. This function returns a file descriptor that can then be used for other file operations.

For instance, formatted data can be written to a file by using the **fprintf** function. This function operates like the **printf** function described in Chapter 5, but the first argument passed to the function is the file descriptor. Its general format is as follows:

```
fprintf(fd,⟨control string⟩,⟨control string arguments⟩);
```

Formatted data can be read from a file using the **fscanf** function, which is similar to the **scanf** function described in Chapter 5. Again, the major difference is that the file descriptor is the first argument passed to the function:

```
fscanf (fd,⟨control string⟩,⟨control string arguments⟩);
```

It is possible to input and output single characters to a file using the I/O functions **getc** and **putc**. These functions require use of a file descriptor, so once a file has been opened by **fopen**, these functions can be used to write or read single characters from the file. For example, if ch is a single character, then the commands:

```
ch = getc (fd);
    and
putc (ch, fd);
```

would be used to read a character from the file or to write a character to the file.

Under most C implementations, the **getc** *function will return a special character when the end-of-file marker is encountered. It is common for this character to be the integer −1. If your implementation supports this feature, it is easy to write a function that returns the contents of a file, character by character, until the EOF marker is found.*

Finally, the function **fclose** is used to close the file. The format for the **fclose** function call is as follows:

fclose (⟨file descriptor⟩);

After this call the file is closed and the file descriptor pointer is freed for other uses.

EXERCISES

1. Write a program that copies one file to a new file, using the UNIX system commands. Be sure to open and close files appropriately.
2. Write a program that copies one file to a new file, using the C primitives. Be sure to open and close files appropriately.
3. Compare the speed of the programs written in Exercises 1 and 2. Test the two programs on files of different lengths and with different types of input (text and numeric).
4. Write a program that prompts the user for a series of filenames and creates a new file with those files merged sequentially in it.
5. Write a program using UNIX system commands to read from one file and create a second file that contains each word on a separate line.
6. a. Modify the program written in Exercise 5 to print out a sorted list of all words in the file. Duplicates should be eliminated.
   b. How might this program be further modified to create a text index or concordance?

APPENDIX 1

Reserved Words in C

When you write C programs, you should avoid using certain C identifiers that have previously specified meanings. These identifiers can be divided into two groups.

One set of reserved words in C is related to data typing. They are the following:

int	struct
float	union
short	extern
long	auto
double	static
unsigned	typedef
char	register

The second set of reserved words is the keywords that would be used in program statements:

if	for
else	return
while	break
do	continue
switch	sizeof
case	entry
default	goto

Most of these words have been previously defined in this book. The following have not been defined:

sizeof: a unary operator that is followed by a variable name and returns the size of the variable value in bytes.

entry: not currently implemented; reserved for future use.

APPENDIX 2

The C Preprocessor

When the UNIX C compiler is invoked by the **cc** shell command, a specified source file is compiled. Actually a number of steps occur during this process, and the first step involves using the C preprocessor.

The C preprocessor is a program that is part of the UNIX environment, and it performs several functions. *Since these functions are so important, virtually all C environments contain some form of a preprocessor.* When the preprocessor is called and your source file is used as input, the preprocessor program scans the contents of the source file. The preprocessor interprets any lines that begin with the # character as command lines, and any such lines cause the preprocessor to take some appropriate action.

There are three major functions for the C preprocessor, invoked by the following command lines:

```
#include    —includes contents of other files
#define     —macro substitution
#if . . .   }
#else . . . }—conditional compilation
#endif      }
```

The **#include** command is followed by a series of filenames, and the effect of this command is to include the contents of those files into the current source file. Most C programs will begin with the preprocessor command line "#include ⟨stdio.h⟩" to include the contents of the standard input-output library into the source file and make those functions available for use. Note that the **#include** command lines (and other preprocessor commands) do not end with a semicolon. Semicolons terminate C program statements, but this is a preprocessor command line, not a program statement per se.

The **#define** command is followed by a series of arguments. The most common use of the **#define** command is to replace an identifier with a token or value throughout the program. For practical purposes, it performs the same sort of function that the Pascal **const** declaration does. For instance, the command line "#define LIMIT 1000" will replace all occurrences of the identifier LIMIT in the program with the value 1000.

A lesser-used function of the **#define** command is to define more complex macro replacements. Instead of simply replacing an identifier with a constant value, it is possible to effectively define one-line functions. For instance, the command line

```
#define cube(a)      (a*a*a)
```

will cause the argument "cube(a)" to be replaced by "(a*a*a)" wherever it occurs.

The C preprocessor's **#define** *command suggests some interesting possibilities. The creative programmer might want to explore how to make C closer to Pascal. For instance, it might be possible to use "#define begin {" and "#define end ;}" as a start—depending on your system, you might find that this will let you replace the braces in C programs with the more familiar* **begin** . . . **end** *constructions.*

The third major use of the preprocessor is to control conditional compilation. Under some conditions, it might be desirable to compile one block of code rather than another. The **#if** . . . **#else** . . . **#endif** construction will let you control this conditional compilation. The **#if** . . . command line contains some condition to be tested. If the condition is true, then the block of code between **#if** and **#else** is compiled; if the condition is false, then the block of code between the **#else** and **#endif** is compiled. One of the major uses of this construction is to control the execution of machine-dependent code. The type of machine in use can be tested. If one machine is in use, one block of code will be compiled; otherwise, an alternative block of code can be used.

APPENDIX 3

C Compilers for Microcomputers

In recent years, a number of C compilers have been developed for use on popular microcomputer systems. Compilers are available for the 8080 microprocessor and its relatives, so microcomputers such as the IBM PC, Apple II (with Z-80 card), or any Z-80-based system can all support the C language.

This appendix provides an alphabetical list (by compiler name) of some of the available compilers. This list summarizes the operating system under which the compiler operates, the cost, and whether the compiler supports the full C language (as described in Kernighan and Ritchie's *The C Programming Language*).

Note: When an entry states that a compiler operates under MS-DOS, it also operates under PC-DOS.

Aztec C
Manx Software, PO 55, Shrewsbury, NJ 07701
Operating system: CP/M-80 Cost: $199
Produces object code. Full implementation of standard C.

BDS C
B. D. Software, PO 9, Brighton, MA 02135
Operating system: CP/M-80 Cost: $150
Produces object code. First C compiler for CP/M.
Large subset of full C, largely follows standard C, with some nonstandard I/O.
Fast compilation and execution.

C/80
Software Toolworks, 14478 Glorietta, Sherman Oaks, CA 91423
Operating system: CP/M-80 Cost: $50

Produces assembly language. Similar to "small-c" compiler; substantial subset of standard C. (As of January, 1984, enhancements have raised this compiler to the level of BDS-C.)

C86
Computer Innovations, 10 Mechanic St, Red Bank, NJ 07701
Operating system: MS-DOS, CP/M-86 Cost: $395
Produces object code. Essentially complete standard C; exception: register variables.

CC86 (Mark Williams' C)
Control-C Software, 6441 SW Canyon, Portland, OR 97221
Operating system: CP/M-86, MP/M-86 Cost: $500
Produces object code. Complete standard C.

C88
Intellect Associates, PO 365, Holbrook, NY 11741
Operating system: MS-DOS, CP/M-86 Cost: $150
Produces object code. Limited subset of standard. Supports only int and char data types, and no structures.

C-Systems C
C-Systems, PO 3253, Fullerton, CA 92634
Operating system: MS-DOS Cost: $195
Produces assembly language. Subset of standard C; no float, cast operation, typedef.

C-Ware C (de Smet C Development Package)
C Ware, 1607 New Brunswick Ave, Sunnyvale, CA 94087
Operating system: MS-DOS, CP/M-86 Cost: $100
Produces object code or assembly language. Good value; large subset of standard C, with fast compilation, linking, execution. Includes screen editor and assembler.

Caprock C
Caprock Systems, PO 13814, Arlington, TX 76013
Operating system: MS-DOS Cost: $35
Limited subset, similar to "small-c." Lacks some control structures (while, for, goto, switch), float, typedef.

de Smet C Development Package
(See C-Ware C)

Digital Research C
Digital Research, PO 579, Pacific Grove, CA 93950
Operating system: CP/M-86, MP/M-86 Cost: $600
Produces object code or assembly language. Essentially complete standard C.

Eco-C
Ecosoft, PO 68602, Indianapolis, IN 46268
Operating system: CP/M-80 Cost: $350
Essentially complete implementation of standard C.

Lattice-C
Lattice Inc, PO 648, Hoffman Estates, IL 60195
Operating system: MS-DOS, CP/M-86 Cost: $500
Produces object code. Full standard C, with fast compilation and efficient code. Rated "superior" in recent comparisons.

Quantum-C
Quantum Software Systems, 7219 Shear Ct, San Jose, CA 95139
Operating system: QNX (included) Cost: $650
Includes QNX (multiuser, multitasking) operating system, provides UNIX-like environment, and includes nearly full UNIX (Version 7) implementation of C.

small-c
Code-Works, Santa Barbara, CA
Operating system: CP/M-80 Cost: (N/A)
Limited subset placed in public domain by Ron Cain ("A small-c compiler for the 8080," Dr. Dobbs Journal, #45). Full upward compatibility with full UNIX C.

Supersoft-C
Supersoft Inc, PO 1628, Champaign, IL 61820
Operating system: (see below) Cost: $500
Produces assembly language. Family of compilers for many microprocessors (including 8080, Z80, 8086, Z8000) and operating systems (CP/M-80, MP/M-86, UNIX, XENIX). Large subset; lacks float, static, typedef, double.

Telecon-C
Telecon Systems, 1155 Meridian, Suite 218, San Jose, CA 95125
Operating system: (see below) Cost: $200
Produces assembly language. Family of compilers for many microprocessors (8080, Z80, 8086, 8088) and operating systems (MS-DOS, CP/M-80, CP/M-86, Flex). Essentially complete standard C; lacks float.

Whitesmith's C
Whitesmiths Ltd., 97 Lowell Rd, Concord, MA 01742
Operating system: CP/M-80 Cost: $750
Produces assembly language for included Whitesmith's assembler. Full implementation of standard C, but some deviation from standard I/O functions.

Mark Williams' C
(See CC86)

APPENDIX 4

C Reference Materials

The following list of materials will provide you with additional information on the topics raised in this book:

The C Programming Language
Brian Kernighan and Dennis Ritchie. Prentice-Hall, 1978.
The standard reference book for C. Elegantly written, it documents the features of the language and provides a programming tutorial for advanced programmers. Appendix A, "The C Reference Manual," defines the language and makes this book a necessity for serious C programmers.

The C Puzzle Book
Alan Feuer. Prentice-Hall, 1982.
A series of C programs that the reader is challenged to decipher. The reader is expected to predict the output (or discover the unexpected outcome) of the code.

"A Comparison of the Programming Languages C and Pascal"
Alan Feuer and Narain Gehani. *Computing Surveys* 14(1): 73–92 (1982).
A technical article that surveys the major differences and similarities between the two languages.

BYTE Magazine. August, 1983.
Each August, *BYTE* devotes an entire issue to a single language, and this issue is devoted to C. The issue contains articles ranging from a C tutorial to a history of UNIX.

The UNIX System
S. R. Bourne. Addison-Wesley, 1983.

A survey of UNIX, with chapters on basic commands, the UNIX editors, and C. Well-written, clear, and concise.

Software Tools in Pascal
Brian Kernighan and P. J. Plauger, Addison-Wesley, 1981.
Explores the concept of software tools, with many excellent examples. Highly recommended.

APPENDIX 5

Annotated Demonstration of a C Program

Background

While C can be used for virtually any programming application, it is often used for systems programming. System programs control the actual machine operations, which are often taken for granted by end-users.

For example, when a user strikes the key marked "A" on the keyboard, it is assumed that the character "A" will appear on the screen. But that might not happen. The computer requires explicit instructions to accomplish that task, and those instructions can be provided in several forms—including an appropriate C program.

This demonstration program illustrates a typical system program. Given a bare machine, such as a PDP 11/23, this program echoes characters to the screen as they are typed on the keyboard. Upon receipt of a carriage return or of 70 input characters, the program prints the number of seconds that elapsed between the time the first and last characters of the line were input.

The program code demonstrates the use of most of the important C constructs that we have discussed in this book. It also illustrates how C program code can be linked to assembly-language routines.

Background on the PDP-11/23

Systems programs often must use information that is specifically linked to the machine upon which the program will run. This program is designed for use on the PDP-11/23, and it uses specific memory locations on that machine.

A brief summary of the locations that will be used follows:

0177560 – address of keyboard status register
0177562 – address of keyboard data register
0177564 – address of screen status register
0177566 – address of screen data register

Each device—the keyboard and the screen—has a status register and a data register. The status registers reflect the current state of the device. Each status register contains a number of bits, which can be set to a value of 1 ("on") or 0 ("off"); the precise bit pattern in the register will determine the state of the device. The data registers store data related to the device; for instance, when a key is pressed on the keyboard, the value of the key pressed is stored in the keyboard data register.

Each device also is assigned an interrupt vector register, which stores the memory location to go to if an interrupt occurs. If an interrupt is generated by a device, the program will jump to some specific action to be taken; the specific action will be determined by the value of the device's interrupt vector.

How does an interrupt occur? The status registers contain two special bits, the READY bit and the INTERRUPT-ENABLE bit. When both bits are set, an interrupt occurs and the CPU transfers program control to the code specified by the interrupt vector.

Basic Program Logic

For both the keyboard and the screen status registers, the INTERRUPT-ENABLE bit starts off set and the READY bit starts off unset. (Thus, no interrupt can occur yet.)

When a user strikes a key, the value of the key is placed in the keyboard data register. In addition, the READY bit on the keyboard status register is set. An interrupt occurs, and program control passes to the location specified by the keyboard interrupt vector. This location is an assembly-language routine which performs a necessary bookkeeping operation and then calls the C function to display the character.

The C function may not be able to display the character on the screen yet; the screen registers may be processing a previous character. The program waits until the screen data register is available, and then transfers the character's value from the keyboard data register to the screen data register. Then an interrupt is triggered and the character is displayed on the screen. (*The PDP 11/23 hardware is hard-wired to display the contents of the screen data register on the screen, so no further instructions are required for that to occur.*)

The program also contains code to handle carriage returns. It generates an automatic carriage return at the end of 70 characters. As an added feature, the program prints the number of seconds taken to enter a line of text.

The program must also manipulate the priorities assigned to various operations. Initially, the CPU has high priority for its operations, and the interrupts generated by keypresses will be unable to interrupt the CPU. To permit a keypress to interrupt the CPU, the priorities of internal CPU operations and the various interrupts must be manipulated as the program executes.

Special Program Operations

This program contains two operations that require further explanation: (1) the use of masks and (2) a special use of structures.

As explained in Chapter 4, it is possible to directly manipulate bit patterns in C with masks. In this program three mask values are defined in the preprocessor section of the code. These are MASK (defined as value 0177), READY (defined as value 0200), and INTENABLE (defined as value 0100).

MASK is used to strip the parity bit from the value of one memory location; when a key is pressed, its ASCII value is stored in the keyboard data register. The most significant bit in this register is a parity bit. To extract the ASCII value alone, the register contents and MASK are logically-anded, and the parity bit is removed.

READY and INTENABLE are used in a similar way. These values are used with logical-ands and logical-ors to either set or turn off specific bits in the status registers.

Structures are used in a special way in this program. In C, it is possible to interpret a specific memory location in several possible ways; for instance, it is possible to interpret a location as either a character or as an integer. In this program, several dummy structures are defined in the variable declaration section of the code, and these are used to permit easy multiple interpretations later in the program.

Program Code

```
/************************************************************************/

/* This program and the associated PDP-11 assembly language routines will take a */
/* character entered at the keyboard of the console of an LSI 11/23 and echo it to the */
/* console screen.                                                                 */

/* After 70 characters have been entered on a line or after a carriage return is entered */
/* at the keyboard, the program prints out the number of seconds (accurate to 0.1 sec- */
/* ond) that have elapsed since the first character on the line was entered.        */

/* The program logic follows:                                                      */
/*        — vectors and counters are initialized                                   */
/*        — keyboard interrupt bit is set                                          */
```

```
/*      — enter an infinite loop, which is broken by an interrupt from the keyboard when  */
/*        a key is hit                                                                    */
/*      — the keyboard interrupt is handled by the C function echo                        */
/*      — when the screen is ready, the screen interrupt bit is set and the screen inter- */
/*        rupt occurs                                                                     */
/*      — the keyboard data is moved to the screen data register, and the character is    */
/*        printed on the screen                                                           */
/*      — if the character is a carriage return or is the 70th character on a line, the C */
/*        function endline prints out the number of elapsed seconds and the string 'sec', */
/*        followed by a carriage return and a line feed                                   */

/*************************************************************************/


/*************************************************************************/

/*                      C preprocessor definitions                       */

/*************************************************************************/

#define PRIOR2 0100                  /* define values for priorities           */
#define PRIOR3 0140
#define KBSTAT 0177560               /* location of keyboard status register   */
#define KBDATA 0177562               /* location of keyboard data register     */
#define KBVEC 060                    /* keyboard interrupt vector              */
#define SCREENSTAT 0177564           /* location of screen status register     */
#define SCREENDATA 0177566           /* location of screen data register       */
#define SCREENVEC 064                /* screen interrupt vector                */
#define CLOCKVEC 0100                /* clock interrupt vector                 */
#define READY 0200                   /* mask to use to set ready bit           */
#define INTENABLE 0100               /* mask to use to set interrupt bit       */
#define MASK 0177                    /* mask to use to clear parity bit        */
#define CR 015                       /* ASCII value for carriage return        */
#define LF 012                       /* ASCII value for line feed              */


/*************************************************************************/

/*                       define global variables                         */

/*************************************************************************/

        int countchar;               /* number of characters on line           */
        int secondcount;             /* number of seconds elapsed on line      */
        char data;                   /* character entered at keyboard          */
```

```
        struct { char kbcharacter;};            /* structures to manipulate          */
        struct { int word1, word2;};            /* the contents of status and        */
        struct { int contents;};                /* data registers                    */


/***********************************************************************/

/* function echo gets keyboard data, checks to see if it is a carriage return or the 70th */
/* character on a line, and echoes the character to the screen if it isn't the end of a line */

/***********************************************************************/
int echo ()
{     extern int countchar;
      extern char data;

      /* if the character is the first character on a line,                  */
      /* initialize the counters                                             */
      if (countchar = = 0)
        secondcount = 0;

      /* count the character                                                 */
      countchar = countchar +1;

      /* get the character from the keyboard data register                   */
      data = KBDATA → kbcharacter;

      /* mask off the parity bit                                             */
      data = (data & MASK);

/* check and see if character is a carriage return or the 70th character on the line. if */
/* not, call the function busywait to handle the display of the character on the screen. if */
/* so, call the function endline to handle the end of the line.                  */

      if ((data != CR) && (countchar != 70))
                busywait();
      else
                endline();

}     /* end function echo                                                   */


/***********************************************************************/

/* function busywait waits for the screen data register to be available. when it is avail- */
/* able, the screen interrupt-enable bit is set, allowing a screen interrupt to occur.    */
```

```
/************************************************************************/
int busywait ()
{   int screenstate;                        /* local var to hold screen status */

/* get the current value of the screen status register. */
screenstate = SCREENSTAT → contents;

/* if the ready bit in the screen status register is off, the screen is busy. wait until the */
/* ready bit is set.                                                                          */

    while (screenstate & READY = = 0)
              {     };

/*  once the ready bit in the screen status register is set, set the interrupt-enable bit, */
/*  and let a screen interrupt happen.                                                      */

    SCREENSTAT → contents = SCREENSTAT → contents | INTENABLE;
                                                                                            */
/*  when the ready bit and the interrupt enable bit are both set, an interrupt will occur. */
/*  it will be handled by the screen interrupt vector which will direct program execution  */
/*  to the assembly language routine interscreen. interscreen will save certain registers  */
/*  and pass control to the C function screenhandler, which actually displays the char-    */
/*  acter on the screen.                                                                    */

  }  /* end function busywait
                                                                                            */


/************************************************************************/

/* function screenhandler moves the data from the keyboard data register to the screen */
/* data register. the LSI 11/23 hardware will then display the data on the screen without */
/* further action required.                                                              */

/************************************************************************/

int screenhandler ()
  {   extern char data;                     /* data in keyboard data register */

    /* turn off the interrupt-enable bit in the screen status register to prevent further */
    /* interrupts until this character has been displayed.                               */

    SCREENSTAT → contents = SCREENSTAT → contents & ~INTENABLE;

    /*move the data which represents the character pressed at the keyboard into */
    /* the screen data register.                                               */

    SCREENDATA → kbcharacter=data;
```

```
    }  /*end function screenhandler                                                    */


/*******************************************************************************/

/* function endline handles the situation which arises when a carriage return or the 70th */
/* character is entered on a line.                                                        */

/*******************************************************************************/

int endline ()
  { int seconds;              /* seconds elapsed entering the line                        */
    int decvalue;             /* the additional tenths of a second                        */
  extern int secondcount;     /* the cpu clock ticks at a rate of 60 per second.          */
                              /* secondcount is imported from function clockcount with    */
                              /* the number of cpu clock ticks which elapsed              */

  /* print a space at the end of the line                                                 */
  data = ' ';
  busywait ();

  /* calculate the number of seconds which elapsed and call function printdigit to out-   */
  /* put the value                                                                        */
  seconds = secondcount/60;
  printdigit (seconds);

  /* print a decimal point                                                                */
  data = '.';
  busywait();

  /* calculate and display the additional tenths of a second which elapsed while enter-   */
  /* ing the line                                                                         */
  decvalue = ((secondcount*10)/60) - (seconds*10);
  data = decvalue + '0';          /* converts the int variable to a char                  */
  busywait();

  /* print the string 'sec' at the end of the line                                        */
  data = ' '; busywait();         /* print a space                                        */
  data = 's'; busywait();         /* print an 's'                                         */
  data = 'e'; busywait();         /* print an 'e'                                         */
  data = 'c'; busywait();         /* print a 'c'                                          */

  /* print a carriage return and line feed for new line                                   */
  data = CR & MASK; busywait();   /* print a carriage return                              */
  data = LF & MASK; busywait();   /* print a line feed                                    */

  /* reinitialize counters for the new line                                               */
  secondcount = 0;
```

```
    countchar = 0;

    } /* end function endline */

/*****************************************************************************/

/* function printdigit uses a recursive call to display the number of seconds which */
/* elapsed while the line was entered.                                              */

/*****************************************************************************/
int printdigit (number)
    int number;                       /* the value to be displayed                  */
    {
        int i;

        if ((i = number/10) != 0)     /* if the number contains > 1 digit           */
          printdigit (i);             /* repeat until only 1 digit left             */

        data = (number % 10 + '0');   /* convert digit to char                      */
        busywait();                   /* display the char                           */

    }   /* end function printdigit                                                  */

/*****************************************************************************/

/* function clockcount uses the cpu clock to count the number of elapsed seconds. the */
/* clock is set to interrupt the program at a rate of 60 interrupts per second. when those */
/* interrupts occur, the clock interrupt vector takes control and directs program flow to */
/* the assembly language routine interclock. interclock passes control to function clock- */
/* count.                                                                                */

/*****************************************************************************/
int clockcount ()
   {
     /* count the number of interrupts, 60 per second                                 */
      ++ secondcount;
   } /* end function clockcount                                                       */

/*****************************************************************************/

/* the main function initiates the program.                                           */
/* it does the following:                                                             */
/*       — sets the interrupt vectors for the kb and screen; when interrupts occur, they */
/*         will then call the right assembly language routines                        */
/*       — lowers the priority of the CPU. initially it is set high, and it must be lowered to */
/*         permit the clock, the keyboard, and screen to interrupt its operations     */
```

```
/*     — the interrupt-enable bit on the keyboard status register is set, to permit an */
/*       interrupt to occur as soon as a key is pressed                                */
/*     — an infinite loop is initiated to wait for the first key to be pressed. when a key */
/*       is pressed, the interrupt which occurs will break the infinite loop           */

/***************************************************************************/
main()
  {
    extern interkb();              /* assembly language routines           */
    extern interclock();           /* which are external to the            */
    extern interscreen();          /* C program                            */
    extern lowprior;

    int kbstate;                   /* store value of keyboard status register */
    int screenstate;               /* store value of screen status register   */

/*  set the jump locations and CPU priorities for handling interrupts from the keyboard, */
/*  screen, and the clock                                                     */

    KBVEC → word1 = interkb;
    KBVEC → word2 = PRIOR3;
    SCREENVEC → word1 = interscreen;
    SCREENVEC → word2 = PRIOR2;
    CLOCKVEC → word1 = interclock;
    CLOCKVEC → word2 = PRIOR3;

/*  lower the priority of the CPU's operations so that interrupts from the keyboard, */
/*  screen, and clock can get in                                              */

    lowprior();

/*  set the interrupt-enable bit on the keyboard status register              */

    kbstate = KBSTAT → contents;           /*get current KBSTAT              */
    kbstate = (kbstate | INTENABLE);       /* set interrupt bit              */
    KBSTAT → contents = kbstate;           /* set KBSTAT to new value        */

/*  begin infinite loop, to be broken by interrupts when a key is pressed     */

    while (1)
      { };
  }   /* end main function                                                    */
```

Assembly Language Routines

To complete the above program, several PDP-11 assembly language routines must be linked to the program. When an interrupt occurs, one of these routines is called to save the current machine state, call the appropriate C function to handle the interrupt, and then restore the machine state afterward. The code for the necessary routines follows:

```
.globl clockcount        /tells assembler that function clockcount is in
                         /a different code module
.globl echo              /tells assembler that function echo is in a dif-
                         /ferent code module
.globl interkb           /permits use of assembly routine interkb in
                         /other modules
.globl lowprior          /permits use of assembly routine lowprior in
                         /other modules
.globl interclock        /permits use of assembly routine interclock in
                         /other modules
.globl interscreen       /permits use of assembly routine interscreen
                         /in other modules

rti = 2

interkb:        mov r0,-(sp)          /save r0
                mov r1,-(sp)          /save r1
                jsr pc, echo          /jump to func-
                                      /tion echo
                                      /in C code
                mov (sp)+,r1          /restore r1
                mov (sp)+,r0          /restore r0
                rti                   /return

mtps = 106400

lowprior:       mov r2,-(sp)          /save r2
                clr r2                /clear r2
                mtps r2               /reset priority
                mov (sp)+,r2          /restore r2
                rts pc                /return

interclock:     mov r0,-(sp)          /save r0
                mov r1,-(sp)          /save r1
                jsr pc,clockcount     /jump to
                                      /clockcount in
                                      /C code

                mov (sp)+,r1          /restore r1
```

```
                mov (sp)+,r0            /restore r0
                rti                     /return

interscreen:    mov r0,-(sp)            /save r0
                mov r1,-(sp)            /save r1
                jsr pc,screenhandler    /jump to
                                        /screenhan-
                                        /dler
                                        /in C code

                mov (sp)+,r1            /restore r1
                mov (sp)+,r0            /restore r0
                rti                     /return
```

Index